HOW TO QUIT LOOKING LIKE A CHRISTIAN AND ACTUALLY BECOME ONE

# THE REAL THING

## DANIELLE TREECE

# THE REAL THING

Scripture quotations are taken from the Holy Bible...(insert Bible statement)

Unless otherwise noted, all Scripture is taken from HOLY BIBLE, NEW INTERNATIONAL VERSION®. Copyright © 1973, 1978, 1984 by International Bible Society. Used by permission of Zondervan Publishing House.

Scripture quotations marked (amp) are taken from the Amplified® Bible, Copyright © 1954, 1958, 1962, 1964, 1965, 1987 by The Lockman Foundation. Used by permission. (www.Lockman.org)

Scripture quotations marked (NKJV) are taken from the New King James Version. Copyright © 1982 by Thomas Nelson, Inc. Used by permission. All rights reserved.

Scripture quotations marked (NLT) are taken from the Holy Bible, New Living Translation, copyright © 1996, 2004, 2007 by Tyndale House Foundation. Used by permission of Tyndale House Publishers, Inc., Carol Stream, Illinois 60188. All rights reserved.

Scripture quotations marked (TLB) are taken from *The Living Bible* copyright © 1971. Used by permission of Tyndale House Publishers, Inc., Wheaton, IL 60189. All rights reserved.

Scripture quotations marked (NCV) are taken from the New Century Version. Copyright © 2005 by Thomas Nelson, Inc. Used by permission. All rights reserved.

Scripture quotations marked (MSG) are taken from *The Message.* Copyright © 1993, 1994, 1995, 1996, 2000, 2001, 2002. Used by permission of NavPress Publishing Group.

Scripture quotations marked (PHILLIPS) are taken from *The New Testament in Modern English*, First American Edition, sixth printing, 1970. Copyright © J. B. Phillips, 1958. Macmillan Publishing Co., Inc., New York.

Scripture quotations marked (KJV) are taken from the Authorized King James Version of *The Holy Bible*, which is in public domain.

Published by
Deep River Books
Sisters, Oregon
http://www.deepriverbooks.com

ISBN-10: ISBN:1937756025
ISBN 13: 9781937756024

Library of Congress: 2012940314

Printed in the USA

Cover design by Dan Yeager, Nu-Image Design

# WHAT DANIELLE TREECE'S STUDENTS ARE SAYING ABOUT *THE REAL THING*

Having over thirty years of experience as a counselor and therapist, I have worked with many young people who seem to be adrift in today's society, who desire closer guidance from their parents, and who need stronger training from their churches. Our youth are facing increasing pressures from the world around them and need foundations rooted in scriptural principles that begin with a personal relationship with Jesus Christ. Being a part of Danielle's first church youth group proved to be a life-changing experience for me, as she led our group through what it meant to have our hearts centered on following Jesus Christ. Through this highly-recommended book, *The Real Thing*, Danielle shares her heart's mission which is to reach, encourage, and train our youth in their quest to live God-centered lives.

**Tony Dettinger, M.Ed., LPC, *Class of 1971***

One small rock thrown in a lake sends ripples twice its own size to every shore of the lake; it grows because it does not stay to itself. Through the ministry, love and guidance of Danielle, I accepted Christ as my Savior in the sixth grade and began my journey of faith. Her teachings and words of wisdom have helped guide me and enabled me to share God's love with others. Her life has been a living example of Christ's love, aimed at young people going through the transition from child to adult. She is an encourager, a giver, a devoted servant, and a rock—always sending ripples of God's love to all.

**Dell Skelton, *Class of 1973***

Danielle Treece taught me how to read the Bible and be inspired by the Word of God. She also taught me how to meditate on scripture and hear from the Holy Spirit. Danielle's passion for experiencing God and living an abundant life in the present resonates with me to this day.

**Glorianne Slovensky, *Class of 2000***

Danielle was my youth spiritual director, growing up in middle school and high school. She was the first real person in my life other than my father who made the Christian faith real to me. Her love for Scripture and her lively application of it created in me a formative faith that has stood with me till this day. Many wise and spirit-filled messages were imprinted upon my heart that I will cherish all the days of my life, until God calls me in glory. I have great faith that Danielle will captivate many more hearts through this book, just as she has done with mine for many years.

Reverend Ryan Andrew Davenport, M.Div., Class of 2004, Central United Methodist Church, Bean Station, TN; Rutledge United Methodist Church, Rutledge, TN

I can't think of anyone that pointed me to Christ more in my teenage years than Danielle Treece. She continually and lovingly gave of her time and wisdom to teach me the Word. Danielle taught me that there is not a sacrifice too great for my Savior or a life sweeter than one lived in obedience to Him. I am continually thankful for her friendship and would encourage anyone who gets the chance to gain from her wisdom and experience.

Karen Hall, *Class of 2005*, Crossway Publishing Company

I highly recommend Danielle's writing to any young person wanting to go deeper in the Lord. She does not stop at mere "head knowledge"; rather, her teaching leads to heart-level revelation and new faith to experience God.

Greg Downs, *Class of 2005*, I.T. business analyst

Danielle has the gift of teaching and a passion for ministering to the hearts of young people, to see the transformed as disciples of Christ. She has challenged me in my own faith journey, to follow Jesus no matter how radical the call.

Casey Ann Erwin, *Class of 2005*, pastor.

What do today's youth need more than anything? God's Word and will in their lives. Danielle Treece communicates this need with precision. Danielle helped shape me into the pastor I am today. Her teaching deeply challenged me as a youth, forcing me to dive deeper into God's Word and seek his will in everything I did.

Harrison J. Bell, *Class of 2006*, pastor, Mt. Carmel United Methodist Church, TN

Danielle taught me that the Bible is the most powerful weapon in a Christian's arsenal to fight the sin, lies, and complacency of the world. She revealed the stunning truth of the verses we dissected and helped me apply it to my daily life, encouraging me to seek the joy of righteousness rather than the fleeting happiness of worldly gain.

**Rachael Miller, *Class of 2010*, pre-ministerial college student**

Hearing Danielle teach is a truly unique experience. Never have I been the subject of a teacher with such a radiating excitement and curiosity for the Word of God. She takes Scripture apart, pulling out the very root of God's message to His people. With Danielle, every line in the Bible plays a part in revealing God's identity and His love.

**Stephanie Brumit, *Class of 2012***

Going into the youth group and realizing that Danielle, an older lady, was my Bible study leader, I thought it would be rather boring. It turns out I was wrong, and she can make her teachings really fun. Once she brought a missionary couple from Nicaragua and their "daughter," which was a big, live tropical parrot.

**Marcy Allen, *Class of 2017***

## WHAT OTHERS ARE SAYING

Danielle Treece's writing reveals her deep faith and her commitment to youth ministry. In *The Real Thing*, she challenges youth to give their hearts fully to an ever-deepening relationship with Jesus Christ, to fulfill God's purpose for their lives.

**Bishop James E. Swanson Sr., Holston Conference of The United Methodist Church**

I love it! An older "youth" who has already navigated the challenges of those young adult years. I admire and trust this young woman whom I have known over forty years. Danielle is a gift to the Church. She is wise, perceptive and practical. Read this and pass it on to others!

**Dr. Robert G. Tuttle, Jr., "The E. Stanley Jones Professor of Evangelism," Asbury Seminary (retired).**

*To every young person God has given me the priceless privilege
to teach, especially our sons Mark, Ben, and John;
and to my husband, Lanny, who is the North Star for our family
and without whom I would never get anything done.*

////////////////////////////////////////////

"Not the labors of my hands can fulfill thy law's demands;
Could my zeal no respite know, could my tears forever flow,
All for sin could not atone;
thou must save, and  thou alone."

**"Rock of Ages, Cleft for Me"**
**A.M. Toplady**
**1776**

# TABLE OF CONTENTS

# PREFACE

As a parent of three sons, I have watched a lot of sports. I genuinely enjoy them and for the most part understand what is going on. I know that as exciting as it is to see a completed pass or touchdown in football, a three-point shot on the basketball court, or a homerun in baseball, nothing has ever been as exciting as it was to watch our son "break from the pack" as a runner. To see him pull ahead and away from the "herd" with stamina and confidence always thrilled my heart.

Having been raised in a traditional church, I was in the pack. I looked like a Christian all the time. I knew about Jesus. Nearly everyone in the herd likes the idea of Jesus. We like His stories, His life and teachings, His healings and miracles, and especially His love. But the idea of really belonging to Him and placing my identity in Him was not taught to me and it was not considered "normal."

As a teenager, I was afraid that God would take something away from me, narrow my life or withhold something good from me, in the same way Eve thought about the fruit in the Garden of Eden.

However, at age eighteen, I came to understand that life actually is about knowing Jesus Christ. Because He is everything you want the most.[1] At a summer camp, the testimony of a popular peer in a bright red hoodie reached me. She pulled away from the pack when she stood up at a campfire to say she had given her life to Christ. I knew that her identity was thereby settled in Jesus because the first thing she did was to tell all of us in the youth group her good news. At that moment I, too, left the herd and entered onto a remarkable new path. The Lord has never narrowed her life nor mine.

Since then the passion of my life is for people like you to really know Him, because I remember too well what it was like to look like a Christian instead of actually being one when I was your age.

In a quick conversation one day with a church friend, I inquired about her daughter who was graduating from high school. She explained how pleased she and her husband were that they had good kids who never gave them any trouble. (Perhaps you might describe your life this way.) "We're really lucky," she said.

After she left, questions burned within me: "But what are your kids passionate about? Do they hunger to know God?"

What about you? What puts fire in your bones? Where is your heart, your passion?

Are you wholly convinced that, according to God's Word, it is far more desirable and profitable to have His wisdom than gold? To have understanding instead of silver? (Proverbs 16:16). Do you know that today He is saying to you, "No eye has seen, no ear has heard, no mind has conceived what God has prepared for those who love Him" (1 Corinthians 2:9)? Are you completely convinced that "Jesus Christ is the same yesterday and today and forever" (Hebrews 13:8)?

> **What about you? What puts fire in your bones? Where is your heart, your passion?**

Or do your priorities reflect little more than "growing rich, increasing the splendor of your house, and living for praise and prosperity" (Psalm 49:16–18)? For at the end of life the question will not be how much you accomplished or achieved or how much money you made. Nor will it be how good you are, how smart, or how often you went to church. Do not settle for half-measures, mediocrity, or the miniscule American Dream. Jesus called this the broad road, travelled by many, travelled by the herd.

God's question will be, "Did you find your way within My Son? Did you place your life in My hands? How much of My Son's character was formed in you?"

To pursue the road that Jesus said "only a few find" (Matthew 7:14, italics mine) requires you to break form the pack. Only then will you discover the life that is "spoilt for everything else but Him."2 Do not settle for less than God's best. Go where the pastors, teachers, and leaders are teaching straighter, stronger, sooner. Because once you really become His, your first thought will be "I wish I had done this sooner!"

One young man described it this way: "Too late loved I Thee, O Thou Beauty of ancient days, yet ever new! Too late I loved Thee!" (Saint Augustine, age 32, AD 354).

Jesus said: "Heaven and earth will pass away, but my words will never pass away" (Mark 13:31).

I am on your team. And I have good news.

---

[1] Jim Rayburn, Founder of Young Life.

[2] Oswald Chambers, *My Utmost For His Highest* (December 23), Barbour and Company, Inc., 1935, copyright renewed 1963.

# CHAPTER 1

# CHANGED AMBITIONS
## *"The Seeking Heart"*

*For now my place is in him ...*
*How changed are my ambitions!*
PHILIPPIANS 3:9-10 PHILLIPS

I sat watching my son play a critical basketball game. With sixty seconds left on the clock, the score was close. Suddenly a player from the opposing team shot and scored a basket on our goal. It counted for our team. We won, and the young man was humiliated.

How easy it is to become disoriented in a fast-paced game. In the same way, the rapid pace of our day can propel you to score mistakenly. Are you certain about the goals you want to score on? Howard Hendricks, a beloved professor at Dallas Theological Seminary, said, "I don't worry that my students will fail. I worry that they will succeed at the wrong things."

## THE SEARCH FOR PURPOSE

Do you often feel that you are furiously sweating and straining your hardest to succeed at life? Beneath your busy routines, do you know for sure why you are here? While our media are flooded daily with new information, the clinics in our schools and on college campuses are likewise flooded with students expressing signs of depression, personal stress, addictions, and contemplations of suicide. For many of you, the inner strength required to deal with your outer pressures too frequently comes up short.

While you are swamped by the "Age of Information," you can still remain ignorant in understanding the purpose of life. Despite the fact that you're busier than ever, it has been said that America's number one social disease is boredom. Information can tell you how to do something, but not why. Time management can tell you how to save thirty minutes, but what do you choose to do with the thirty minutes you just saved? You can log on to the Internet to acquire facts on any subject, but where do you go to find wisdom to apply the facts?

## IS THAT ALL THERE IS?

Perhaps you can identify with this young man whose father wanted to talk to him about the goals of life.

"Son, you're getting up in your teens now, and I want you to go to college so you can get a good job, so that you can make enough money to live where you want to live, buy what you want to buy, and drive what you want to drive."

"Let me make sure I understand," the son said. "You want me to go to college so I can get a good job and have enough money to live where I want to live, buy what I want to buy, and drive what I want to drive. Right?"

"I think you've got it."

" But why am I doing that?" he asked, puzzled.

His father seemed at a loss for a moment. He had explained himself clearly, he thought. "Well, it's very simple, Son. I want you to go to college, so you can get a good education, so you can have a good job so that you can drive what you want to drive, buy what you want to buy, and live where you want to live. That way, when you get married and have your children, you will have enough funds to be able to send them to college so they can get a good job and live where they want to live, buy what they want to buy, and wear what they want to wear." He sat back, satisfied that he had been clear.

"But Dad," the son began, the furrows between his brows even deeper this time. "Why am I doing all that?"

His father sighed heavily and added, "So that your children, when they grow up, can go to college, and get a good education, secure good jobs so that they will have enough money to live where they want to live, wear what they want to wear, and buy what they want to buy. That way, when you retire, you will not have to depend on Social Security, but you'll be able to live out your golden years with ease, maybe travel around the world. You won't be oppressed by the financial limitations of the times, or dependent on the ability of others to pay into Social Security."

The son, now as exasperated as his father, threw up his hands and said, "But why am I doing all that?"

The father, not knowing anything else to say, finally just shouted, "Go to school now!"[1]

The only goal the father knew was to acquire as much from life, as soon as you can, so you can be secure. It was clear to him that you simply head as fast as you can to the finish line in pursuit of prosperity.

But is that all there is? It wasn't enough for the son. He wanted to know the *purpose* for having prosperity. When you have everything, do you know what it is for?

His father didn't have an answer. He had information without understanding. The psalmist says that a person who has prosperity without understanding is like the beasts of the field that simply live and die. (See Psalm 49:20.)

**Get Real:**

When you have everything, will you know what it is for?

## EMPTY PROSPERITY

This story illustrates that prosperity as a goal in itself will not satisfy. When the benefits of life become the point of life, you risk living in spiritual poverty. If all those around you are bowing down to things created instead of the Creator, they are unknowingly scoring on lesser, secondary goals.

I know how you long for true Christian friends. I know many of you are disillusioned at the way people who profess to be Christians go out and live like everyone else, without a second thought. "We suppose that we live in a Christian society! How we fool ourselves. We live in a world that gives little value to spiritual things unless they produce material results."[2]

Research reveals that fewer than ten percent of church-going Christians base their important life decisions on God and His will. "In other words, more than ninety percent decide on the basis of their own intelligence, peer opinion, whim, or fancy. They marry people and move to new cities without so much as a ten-minute prayer."[3]

This failure to live according to biblical truth has produced a "whatever" generation where each person lives by what seems "right in his own eyes," much like the nation of Israel in Judges 21:25 where "everyone did as he saw fit." Proverbs 16:25 gives us the outcome of that philosophy: "There is a way that seems right to a man, but in the end it leads to death."

## GOALS THAT SEEM RIGHT

Some common goals people choose to pursue as a purpose for life are:

### 1. To be successful, to arrive at the top.

For many, worth and significance is found in their achievements and abilities to perform at high levels. This can start as early as Little League and awards day in elementary school. The achiever begins to build his life on his own competence. In contrast, the person who is not at the top can begin to sense at an early age that he doesn't measure up.

### 2. To do more.

Our fast-paced society pressures all of us to demand more and more of ourselves. The success of a day is measured by how many activities you can pack into your schedule or check off the to-do list. Bookstores are flooded with time-management materials designed to help you get more done in less time. I have observed that busy-ness has become the defining characteristic for American people who are always asking "How can I do more?" Yet the wiser question for us to ask would be: "Am I doing the right thing?"

### 3. To have more.

The whole basis of advertising is to make us dissatisfied and discontent with what we have—so we'll go out and buy more! This desire for more is never satisfied. But like the story above, the purpose of doing more is so you can have more. Thus, life begins to become like a game of Monopoly. You just keep passing "Go" in your pursuit to acquire more. Whether it's leisure, adventure, entertainment, or material possessions, the goal has become to perform well, so you can have what you want, so you can do what you want.

## 4. To pursue pleasure.

Feeling good, having a good time, is a primary value for many people. Is this big enough to be the goal of life—the reason to choose one activity over another? Today, anything that interferes with pleasure is viewed as unnecessary, unwanted, and something to be avoided. Many people work in order to play and to make enough money to pursue recreational activities they consider fun.

Your generation is currently the most entertained one to have ever lived. Through the endless options of cell phones, iPhones, computer games, BlackBerry apps, and cable stations, idle pleasure has no limit. Even at school and church, many of your friends just want to be entertained. This is the new normal and a popular little "god."

## 5. To pursue knowledge and a good education.

Clearly this is a highly valuable and significant goal. While a good education certainly *serves* the goal of your life, it is not big enough to *be* the goal of your life. This would mean that a person without a full education, like the world-renowned Dwight L. Moody, who only finished fifth grade, or a tribal jungle man, or a mentally impaired person, could never attain the goal or win the race. While knowledge is a profitable benefit, it falls short as the purpose to life. Knowledge can only be as valuable as the understanding you bring to it and the way you choose to use it. The map needed for life is found in wisdom far beyond what our humanistic educational systems provide.

## 6. To be a "good person."

This prominent American goal seems very worthwhile. Indeed there is great value in seeking to be good. Yet for too many of us this means the pursuit of a nice middle-class life where you obey the law, don't cause trouble, try to be nice to others, and make some sort of contribution with your time and abilities. As a young woman recently said, "I used to be like the silverware in the drawer, all nice and shiny and neatly lined up in the proper slots."

Again, for a human being created in the image of God, this goal is too small. The American Dream is not big enough to satisfy the heart designed for God. If you place your worth in your own self-effort and moral uprightness, then how good do you have to be? Whose standard of what is "good" do you choose to live by? A person can be viewed as good yet not even believe in God. Such people credit themselves, not God, for their goodness and their blessings. Jesus said that only God is good (Matthew 19:17). Do we really want to be so prideful as to call ourselves "good"? True goodness comes only as a by-product of a relationship with God whose purpose is remake me in His image per His original plan.

## Truth is...

### The American dream is not big enough to satisfy the heart designed for God.

### 7. To find ourselves, refine ourselves, and fulfill ourselves.

One of the largest sections in bookstores is the "self-help" or "about me" section. I am all about learning new things that will improve or enhance my life. Yet while it is always helpful to improve yourself, this again is not big enough to be the goal of life. As a Christian, beware of anything that makes you self-indulgent—no matter how good it sounds. Our self-indulgent culture has caused many people to cling tenaciously to rights they believe they are entitled to have. Yet again, this worldview is skewed because Jesus, "who though He was God, did not demand and cling to his rights" (Philippians 2:7 TLB).

## GAINING UNDERSTANDING

The wisest man of Greece, Socrates, said the secret to mastering life was to "know thyself." The wisest man of Rome, Marcus Aurelius, said the secret to mastering life was to "control thyself." But it took the wisest man of Galilee, Jesus, to state that the true and lasting path for mastering life is found in the two words "deny thyself."[4] The biblical path to finding yourself is to lose it. (See Matthew 16:24–25.)

The truth is that the goal of life isn't about you or me at all. It's about Him. "He [Jesus] died for all, that those who live should no longer live for themselves but for Him" (2 Corinthians 5:15). Goals that keep self at the center miss the mark, God's mark. Neither will they satisfy. God yearns for you to understand that your life won't work properly until you turn the affections of your heart away from self and back to Him, as they were in the Garden of Eden.

## CHANGED AMBITIONS

Living without understanding. Missing the goal. It happened so easily to a young man named Saul. In Scripture he describes how he based his identity on every goal illustrated above. He was highly esteemed for his fine family background, his impeccable education, and moral ethics, for his detailed knowledge of religious laws, for his outstanding achievements, and zeal for his Jewish faith.

Yet after a decisive encounter face to face with the risen, living Christ, Saul (whose name God changed to Paul) passionately proclaims, "How changed are my ambitions!" after he tells us the reason: "For now my place is in him." (See Philippians 3:9–10 PHILLIPS.) He describes his former life as "useless rubbish," "refuse," and "dung," *compared* to the all-surpassing value of knowing Jesus Christ and being found in Him. From that point on, his heart and his life's identity was found in Jesus.

## GOD'S GOAL FOR YOU

The greatest commandment is "to love the Lord your God with all your heart and with all your soul and with all your mind and with all your strength" (Mark 12:30). If you want your life to be God-centered, you must return God to His rightful place. He is God; you are not. There is nothing difficult or complex about understanding this. The difficultly is in doing it.

This great little man, Saul, became the great apostle Paul—missionary, and writer of much of the New Testament, who has impacted Christians for more than 2,000 years by clarifying the goal for life: You do not stop at believing in and receiving His Son; You desire to journey on, to adhere your life's identity in Him, in order to become like Him. And why? Because God created us to bring glory and honor to Him, not self.

Paul writes, "He [God] chose them [us] to become like his Son" (Romans 8:29 NLT). The purpose of your salvation is for all that is within you to serve Him, for your identity to be placed and settled in Him. As Paul wrote to believers back then, so he speaks to you today: "Oh, my dear children! I feel as if I am going through labor pains for you again, and they will continue until Christ is fully developed in your lives" (Galatians 4:19 NLT).

You want to look more like Him each day. Since Paul had no hesitation about expecting to see the people in the churches he planted grow into the likeness to Jesus, you can be assured that God's call for you is to do the same thing today.

While many of you may immediately react that this is impossible, God says that this is "not too difficult for you or beyond your reach" (Deuteronomy 30:11). God was well-pleased with Jesus before He ever left home, preached a sermon, healed a sick person, walked on water, or died on the cross! (See Luke 3:22.) So what pleased God?

Jesus honored God in all that He did in the simple everyday life of his village. Learning the trade of a carpenter, He would have become head of the family when His father died. "Jesus became wiser and grew physically. People liked him, and he pleased God" (Luke 2:52 NCV). His life's identity was found in His heavenly Father. We know that at age twelve when His family went to the Temple for Passover, He lingered to talk with the religious teachers who were amazed at his questions and wisdom (Luke 2:46–47).

## A KIND OF SHOCK

I vividly recall the first time I heard this truth. I was in my mid-twenties, working for a church. A group of us went to lunch to get acquainted with our new pastor. As we piled into a warm car flooded with light from the April sun, we had lots of chatter as different conversations went on at the same time. At one point, the pastor's wife turned to me with a genuine smile, a light in her blue eyes, and quietly said, "We are just two common people seeking to be more like Jesus every day."

I was floored. I had never heard anyone speak so plainly and so clearly "un-muddied" about their purpose in life. To be honest, I was somewhat put off. That agenda just wasn't quite sophisticated enough for me. It was too simple and too pious. Thus I quickly dismissed her comment.

But I never forgot it. That bright afternoon her words planted a seed of reality within my spirit. As months, years, and many experiences passed, tiny tendrils began to sprout from this truth, began to grow until it gripped me with a stunning reality. She was right. It really was that simple. And it wasn't pious at all because it is the most humbling goal a person could ever have!

It shouldn't have taken me so long to see the truth, because it only took me a split second to recognize that she bore "the light of life" in her blue eyes.

## THE IMPACT OF THIS GOAL

Placing your identity in Jesus is not an easy call. It must be accompanied by one of those warnings on television that say, "Do not try this on your own!" If you try to become more like Christ on your own, you will burn out and give up in defeat. Only God can deposit the gift of the Holy Spirit into your life to change your heart. No one can do this without complete dependence on God Himself.

Also, you will find that it is often not popular, comfortable or convenient to belong to Jesus because it is totally countercultural. Multitudes of voices encourage you to believe that everyone has a different God and that really they are all the same. Our society promotes advertisements that declare "you deserve this ...," so pamper and indulge self. You will be misunderstood, laughed at, or even rejected.

Paul compared this choice to the devotion of an athlete in vigorous training. Athletes who compete at the Olympic level find their identity totally changed. Their orientation to life is completely different from other people. Because of this goal, they have a basis for choosing one value over another instead of choosing what simply "seems right" to them.

Unlike the son in the opening story, they know that now every part of their life converges to one single center, and even better, they know now *why* they are expending all of themselves. Now the larger objective determines every other decision, no matter how small: what to do, where to go, what to eat, when to get up, and when to sleep—maybe even where to live.

This is what happened to Paul. He was not given a new set of rules to live by but a new center to which his heart converged. His identity was with Jesus. He could now say with confidence, "I do not run like a man running aimlessly" (1 Corinthians 9:26).

The same thing can happen to you. The point to each daily activity is that He would increase and you would decrease, thus serving His kingdom instead of your own. You also will come to discover that seeking "God does not narrow one's life but brings it, rather, to the level of highest possible fulfillment."[5]

## HOW DOES IT WORK?

God does not want to change your personality or to make you a religious robot. There is no one else made like you, and He has a unique plan that only you can fulfill for Him. You still pursue your passions, your education, talents, hobbies, and interests the same as anyone else, but now He wants you to use all of these things for Him, to know *what* to do with all you have.

If you love playing a sport, for you God is all over that sport. Recently an NFL player has been both praised and criticized for honoring God above all in his football career. He has used his fame to minister to children suffering with illnesses. If you are avid about your academics, ask God to give you His thoughts and His true wisdom and seek His direction for the best way to use the intelligence and skills He has given you. If you have a great love for people and want to be with them most of the time, ask God to show you how to best use your gifts to serve others for Him. Usually, whatever you love the most is what God wants you to do. He made you that way for a reason.

The goal is the same. Now your ambitions belong to Him and "whatever you do, put your whole heart and soul into it, as into work done for the Lord, and not merely for men" (Colossians3:23 PHILLIPS). Even the details.

## A LIFELONG PROCESS

Once you come to belong to Him, He will begin the process of forming God's likeness within you. His thoughts will start to become your thoughts, His reactions your reactions, His plans your plans. When God's love is written on your heart and mind, self will begin to decrease and you will gradually increase your capacity to love others more and to depart from un-Christlike attitudes, speech, and reactions.

And there is no circumstance you will ever face in which you cannot become more like Jesus. Understanding this makes every day come alive with exciting opportunities and challenges that bring joys you can't even imagine.

Here is a letter written recently by a young man at our church:

> This is my story of faith to another youth. When I was born, my Mom and Dad were doing good. When I turned four they turned around; they started doing drugs and we stopped going to church. Then my Grandpa and Grandma took me in because my Dad started to abuse me. He hurt me and if they didn't stop I would go to an orphanage so they took me and my six-month-old brother. Then I started to go to a church I didn't like so I came to another church until I found Mafair and have been here ever since.
>
> But my walk with Christ didn't really start until this year when I went to Bancroft Bible Camp. At chapel we all closed our eyes and were asked to raise our hands if we needed a stronger bond with Jesus. I raised my hand and that night my sixteen-year-old counselor took me outside and talked to me and answered my questions about Christ. This is my story of faith.
>
> Your friend,<br>Tanner O'Neal
>
> P.S. Faith is not just for young people. I'm 12 and JESUS IS EVERYTHING.

Two thousand years ago, Paul wrote the same words this way: "I'm not saying that I have this all together, that I have it made ... By no means do I count myself an expert in all of this, but I've got my eye on the goal ... and I'm not turning back" (Philippians 3:12–14 MSG). It is not great talent that God blesses, but likeness to Jesus.

As Paul stated in Ephesians 1:11: "It's in Christ that we find out who we are and what we are living for" (MSG).

[1] Dr. Tony Evans, "The Meaning of Life" (tape).

[2] Morton Kelsey, *Faith at Work*, Magazine Fall 1996, 10.

[3] Jim Cymbala, *Fresh Faith*, Zondervan Publishing, 1999, 77.

[4] Glenn Clark, *I Will Lift Up Mine Eyes*, Harper & Row, 1937, 47.

[5] A.W.Tozer, *The Pursuit of God*, Christian Publications, 1982, 6.

# CHAPTER 2

# FOUND IN HIM

### *"A New Heart"*

*You should not be surprised at my saying,
'You must be born again.'*
**JOHN 3:7**

I n 1924 the New York Giants played the Washington Senators in the World Series. Each team had won three games and the seventh game was played in Washington. After eight innings the game was tied at three. The New York fans stood as their team came to bat. But it was three up and three down. They grew quiet as Washington came to bat. It was two up and two down. The fans stood with anxious eyes as Leon "Goose" Goslin came to the plate.

On the fifth pitch, he knocked the ball far down between center and left field. The ball hit the fence and ricocheted off. "Goose" was quickly motioned around the bases by the coach. The shortstop dropped the throw from the outfield and the runner made a mad dash for home plate. It was a close tag, but everyone knew he was safe!

Suddenly, however, there was a roar in the stands as fans saw the umpire with his thumb in the air, saying, "Out!" The Washington crowd was livid. They knew he was safe!

The umpire advanced to the megaphone, "Ladies and gentlemen, the runner is out. He is out because he failed to touch first base."[1] While it appeared to the onlookers in the stands that the runner had won the game, the official knew that in reality he had not scored at all because he sped past first base without making contact. He missed what was essential.

In the same way, being a real Christian also requires an essential first base. It is not true that everyone is going to heaven. Each of us must come to a turning point where we fully see our sinfulness and agree with God that it is real. We leave the broad road we've been on and begin to travel the narrow road Jesus spoke of in Matthew 7:13–14. The only way you can become His is to be born again, not of the flesh, but of the Spirit.

## APPEARANCE VS. REALITY

Just as the crowd mistakenly thought the winning run in the World Series was a cinch, a similar mistake can occur in the Christian life. It is the error of looking like a Christian instead of being one.

On the outside we may appear as though we're doing great. You can be a good person, involved in church activities that serve God and everyone believes you are a Christian. Yet in reality, only you know whether or not you are actually experiencing a personal relationship with Jesus Christ.

Appearances are all-important for lots of people. Whether it's the way we want to look—wearing certain labels, working out daily, or driving a certain car—most of us invest time, energy and money to have a certain image. You know people who starve themselves, tan themselves, lift weights, color their hair, tint their contacts, and bleach their teeth to feel good about how they look.

So it's easy to see how this emphasis on appearance can spread to your Christian walk. Too many have been taught how to look and act like a Christian instead of being taught how to truly be one. Nothing is more exhausting than cosmetic Christianity. Trying to keep up appearances, when your heart isn't in it, is tiring and boring.

## MEET A SEEKER

The Gospel of John tells us about a man who spent his entire life living this way. After years of being the perfect, respected leader in his religious community, Nicodemus was weary of pursuing lesser goals, all the "dos and don'ts." Deep within, he knew he was missing something essential.

He had heard about a powerful new prophet and teacher and had even observed His ability to perform miracles. One night Nicodemus sought out a secret meeting with Jesus because he feared the disfavor of the other Pharisees. He approached Jesus with respect and caution.

Jesus saw beyond the appearances to his heart. In essence He said, "Nicodemus, you've done it all. You've performed well, been a great team player, and scored many times. But none of that counts toward the goal because you have never actually touched first base. Touching first base means that you must be born again." (See John 3:1–21.)

Notice that Jesus answered a question Nicodemus didn't actually ask! He knew that Nicodemus did not have authentic salvation. "I tell you the truth … flesh gives birth to flesh, but the Spirit gives birth to spirit. You should not be surprised at my saying, 'You must be born again'" (John 3:5–7).

Duh?

Nicodemus had no clue what Jesus meant, no comprehension of what it meant to be "born again." He thought he had to literally re-enter his mother's womb. "'You are Israel's teacher,' said Jesus, 'and do you not understand these things?'" (John 3:10).

Despite the fact that he was a highly educated, prominent religious leader, Jesus had to repeat Himself twice. With some embarrassment, Nicodemus suddenly realized that Jesus was imparting a spiritual truth, not a physical one. But he still had no idea what it meant.

## CHRISTIAN APPEARANCES THAT DON'T SATISFY

First, Nicodemus was striving so hard to be right. It is a great temptation to think that the goal of life is to be right. Yet this can become a source of pride, breeding a critical spirit, a superior attitude, or an uncaring heart. You can do right things with a wrong spirit.

Paul Little, a Christian writer, shares why this is not enough. He illustrates levels of faith that will not satisfy. One of these is indoctrination faith. With this kind of faith, people are well-trained from the early years to know all the right answers, to seldom miss church, to win Bible quizzes. They use all the right words, but they have mistakenly identified the defining mark of a Christian as right behavior. But looking like a

Christian does may not mean you are one. Jesus said, "Not all who sound religious are really godly people. They may refer to me as 'Lord,' but still won't get to heaven" (Matthew 7:21 TLB ).

Next, Nicodemus was striving to be religious. A second level of faith can be described as conformity faith. While you can appear to others to be a good Christian, your behavior often has nothing whatsoever to do with truly knowing God personally. This kind of faith is primarily the result of strong Christian surroundings. "[You] may do all the right things and none of the wrong things—but only because of the external pressure of family and church."[2] The driving desire is to conform to please family and friends.

While you can absorb Christian values from your environment, this does not mean that you are a Christian. Too frequently, once the environment changes, your behavior may also change. When you leave home or go off to college, your faith will likely not go with you if your identity was conformed to a Christian environment instead of the person of Jesus Christ.

Lastly, Nicodemus was striving to be respectable. This is called comfortable faith. You want to be a Christian as long as it is convenient, comfortable and doesn't disturb the status quo. This kind of casual Christianity produces respectable, church-going members who believe religion should be kept in its place. It is not to interfere with the real values of life like personal peace and prosperity. You are not sure you want to serve a God who might require you to sacrifice time, comfort, convenience or money, or lead you to get involved with unlovable people. It isn't a real option.

Nominal Christianity has become such a cultural norm that the vast majority of churchgoers remain content to name the name of Christ, yet have little desire to go any deeper with God. They settle for respectability, never pursuing a relationship of getting to know Jesus as a living reality. However, we learn from Nicodemus that settling for the secondary will not satisfy.

## FIRST BASE

Jesus told Nicodemus that he must experience saving faith. Saving faith is more than outward conformity to cultural Christianity; it is a radical *attachment* to the person of Jesus Christ. When scripture says to "believe" in the Lord Jesus Christ, it means more than mental agreement. The word in Greek means to "give yourself up to Him, take yourself out of your own keeping and entrust yourself into His keeping ..." (Acts 16:31 AMP). You are saved when you actually entrust your entire life to His lordship.

## SAVING FAITH IS ABOUT REBIRTH

Only when you are born of the Spirit, born from above, do you experience saving faith. As Jesus stated, this rebirth is not optional. It is as essential to your life as first base is to baseball.

## ARE YOU ALL HERE?

Without rebirth, you are only two-thirds here.

Despite the precious little bundle that you were at birth, all of us were born missing a part. Really? The body comes in, kicking, screaming, wrinkled and hungry; and our soul comes in, cooing, crying, smiling, soothed by touch and comfort. But the spirit within all of us is dead, just as it was in Nicodemus.

No way! How? Why?

When God placed Adam and Eve in the Garden of Eden they had complete fellowship with Him. It was in man alone that God placed the spiritual image of Himself by His very own breath. The paradise they lived in had no suffering, no illness, no sadness, not even any death. It was paradise. All God asked them to do was obey one command: "You are free to eat from any tree in the garden; but you must not eat from the tree of the knowledge of good and evil, for when you eat of it you will surely die" (Genesis 2:16–17).

But when tempted by Satan, Adam and Eve did choose to disobey and eat from the tree. Since God had warned this would bring death, what died? They did not immediately fall dead physically. (However, at this moment, physical death, which previously had no claim on them,

**Truth is...**

**Saving faith is a radical attachment to the person of Jesus Christ.**

did enter the human race. From this moment on, every person would at some point die.)

Likewise, their souls made up of their mind, will, and emotions did not die because now they are contaminated with guilt, self-justification, and shame.

It was their spirit, the part of them that had unbroken fellowship with God, that died at that moment. Because God is completely sinless and holy, their sin has now severed their ability to live in fellowship with Him.

## AN UNCOMFORTABLE TRUTH

As a devout Hebrew, Nicodemus should have known this, but like many people, he missed it. He didn't understand that we are all born into a predicament because we are born with a fallen, sinful nature.

I hear you yelling in protest. You've just recently held a new baby and say "no way" does that baby have a fallen nature! Most people simply do not really believe this. I didn't believe it either. I argued with my best friend for years over this issue. I thought she was crazy and morbid.

Popular thought today wants you to believe that all human beings are born basically good. This is illustrated by a bumper sticker I saw recently which said "Born OK: The First Time." Secular, humanistic psychology teaches that you enter this life "neutral." All you have to do is nurture yourself, educate yourself, and you will gradually evolve into a good person.

However, the Bible professes a uniquely different worldview of man. Dr. David Seamands, professor, minister, and counselor has summarized it this way:

"God has revealed to us in His Word that we do not enter this life morally neutral. Rather, we are victims of a basic tendency toward evil, a proclivity toward the wrong. We call it original sin ... We do not come into this world perfectly neutral, but imperfectly weighted in the direction of the wrong. We are out of balance in our motives, desires, and drives. We are out of proportion, with a bent toward the wrong. And because of this defection our natures, our responses are off-center." [3]

## REALLY GOOD NEWS

What? Yes, this actually is great news. Because now you no longer have to feel like you are the worst person in the world because everyone else is just as bad as you and me! "We are *all* [italics mine] infected and impure with sin" (Isaiah 64:6 TLB). Paul reiterates the thought: "All have sinned and fall short of the glory of God" (Romans 3:23). No one is different. Sin is not a defect. It is a condition we are born into, and it is a fact.

You already know this anyway don't you? You know how sinful, selfish, and small you can be. And now you know why! Isn't this a relief? Has anyone had to teach you to want your own way, to get angry or demanding? Has anyone had to teach you to focus on what you want more than anything else? No. This is simply the reality of your human condition. Your behavior is off-center because your inborn, inherited nature is off-center.

See, when your parents got married, it was one sinner marrying another sinner. And when you came along, as well as your siblings, you simply added to the number of sinners in your family. Hmmmm … that explains a lot, doesn't it? From birth, every human being, including you, is tainted by the stream of humanity that came before them.

Since God Himself is spirit, the only way He can communicate with you is through your spirit. Now Adam and Eve no longer had a way to communicate with God. In the same way that a dead person cannot smell brownies, a person who is spiritually dead cannot comprehend the things of God! His receptor is broken. That is why Nicodemus was in a fog bank.

## THE GOOD NEWS OF SAVING FAITH

"Oh, what a terrible predicament I am in! Who will free me …? Thank God! It has been done by Jesus Christ our Lord. He has set me free" (Romans 7:24–25 TLB). Only God.

The only way the spirits of Adam and Eve could be "made alive" again (Ephesians 2:5) was to let God to deal with their sin. The fig leaves they used to cover themselves did not cut it. So God personally clothed them Himself with the skins of an animal, likely a lamb. This required taking the life of an innocent lamb and the shedding of its blood.

## "I'VE GOT YA' COVERED"

Nicodemus would have sacrificed many lambs at the temple to atone for his sins. Yet in spite of his extensive religious experiences, he could not connect the dots. Thus, right in the middle of Jesus' conversation with Nicodemus, are the words, "For God so loved the world that he gave his one and only Son, that whoever believes in him shall not perish but have eternal life" (John 3:16). God provided a way where there was no way. The Gospel writers refer to Jesus as the "Lamb of God, who takes away the sin of the world" (John 1:29) because He became the final lamb that ever had to die for sin.

Whatever fig leaves you're relying on—lay them aside. The only righteousness you or I will ever possess is that which is given by the Lamb of God.

In Exodus God instructed the Hebrews to slay a lamb, to cover the sides and tops of their doorframes with blood so that God's judgment, the angel of death, would pass over them. "And when I see the blood, I will pass over you" (Exodus 12:13).

The cross is the new and final Passover. Because when He sees the blood of His Lamb over the doorpost of your heart, He says you are covered and fully perfect in Him—forever.

## CHRIST IN YOU

Now it is possible to "do what Jesus would do" because you will begin to think as He thinks and see as He sees. His Spirit now lives within you. He says "I will give you a new heart and put a new spirit in you … I will put my Spirit in you and move you to follow my decrees and be careful to keep my laws" (Ezekiel 36:26–27).

A high school girl at our church recently shared that one of the first things she noticed after she was born again was that for the first time ever, foul language began to offend her. She was astonished that she no longer wanted to speak it or hear it. Now, "instead of redoubling our own efforts, [we] simply embrace what the Spirit is doing in us" (Romans 8:4 MSG).

## WHO TOLD ME?

Tony Campolo asks, "If God had a great big wallet filled with the pictures of His children, do you know for *sure* that your picture is there?"

Like Nicodemus, as a teenager I went through all the motions of being a good, religious person. I held high youth council offices in my state and looked like a great Christian. I never did anything that would be considered morally wrong.

But I did not have the assurance that I was fully His or that my picture was in God's wallet. Because I had settled for lesser goals, I knew I had not been born of His Spirit. Three weeks before going to college, I found myself sitting around a blazing campfire at a church camp. A popular peer stood up to say that she had met Jesus as a personal friend and had given her life to Him. I was blown away. She had everything a girl could want! Why would she want Jesus more? Her red hoodie and blonde hair are as clear today as they were then.

As she spoke, I knew this was the real thing. Her wholehearted, authentic love for Jesus spilled forth upon me and I wanted more. Her life was never to be the same, and neither was mine.

He doesn't ask you if you believe that He is Savior "of the world." Even the demons believe that. His question is: "Am I your personal Savior?" The next morning, on a pier overlooking a river, I too was re-born from above. It was not an emotional decision. I just mentally agreed with God and His verdict on my sinful nature; I agreed that the only remedy was His death on the cross. After all, if I'm okay and you're okay, then why would He have to die on a cross?

## Get Real:

**She had everything a girl could want! Why would she want Jesus more?**

That morning I went to breakfast, knowing for sure that my picture was in God's wallet, that now I really knew Him. How awesome that Almighty God personally spoke to me and invited me to become His child! He will do the same for you. "For his Holy Spirit speaks to us deep in our hearts, and tells us that we really are God's children" (Romans 8:16 TLB). This is when you receive complete assurance that He is now in you, and you know that you know that you know.

## GETTING OUT OF THE DUGOUT

Jesus explained that the majority of people won't make this decision. He said, "For wide is the gate and broad is the road that leads to destruction, and many enter through it. But small is the gate and narrow the road the road that leads to life, and only a few find it" (Matthew 7:13–14). Instead of coming to know Him, they remain content to fine-tune the two-thirds of life they understand.

I have actually witnessed parents and ministers discourage young people from seeking more, considering them to be overboard or fanatic. They don't see a need for their child to actually know or be identified with Jesus.

I once heard a young man try to share with his father the fact that he had recently been born again. The father immediately denied it with a pat on the shoulder saying, "You don't mean that! Why you've been in church all your life!" The father mistook appearance for reality. I've had a parent tell me her teen was spending "too much time at the church" and she was afraid her daughter would not be "balanced."

Yet I have also seen young people boldly step out in saving faith when no one else in their family would. And from observation of those students, I say, "No eye has seen, no ear has heard, no mind conceived what God has prepared for those who love him" (1 Corinthians 2:9). Not one of these young people has ever turned back, nor had a moment's regret. In fact, many have won some of their family members to Christ.

## CHANGED AFFECTIONS

Have you ever seen a news clip of someone who kept talking after they thought the microphone was off? Aren't we shocked to hear them say something totally opposite of the person we thought they were? Jesus said that "… out of the overflow of the heart the mouth speaks" (Matthew 12:34). He knew that the ways we speak won't change until our heart does.

When you are born again, your new heredity will bring new "want tos." Now your "want to" begins to come into alignment with your "ought to." You no longer have to cover up or rationalize the things in you that are not of God. Now that's a relief, isn't it? Instead you simply agree with His verdict, saying "this is sin."

Our son who worked on staff with Campus Crusade for Christ shares a unique and moving story. One Easter, pastor Rene Schlaepfer of Twin Lakes Church in Aptos, California, rented a casino for the day to hold an evangelistic service. They also hired an Easter Bunny for the children. At the close of the service, the "Easter Bunny," with his big plastic smiling head on the outside, was "born again" with sobbing on the inside. He went down to the front to kneel to receive Jesus. But he did not remove his head out of respect for the children.

Your new nature—born from above—desperately wants to know Him, love Him, and settle your identity in Him. "I run in the path of your commands, for you have set my heart free" (Psalm119:32).

## ALL HERE

Now you are not only in God's wallet, but you also know you are "all here," body, soul, and the very Spirit of God Himself.

In 1552, Martin Luther described it this way: "Faith is a divine work in us, which changes us and makes us newly born of God, and kills the old Adam, makes us completely different men in heart, disposition, mind and every power, and brings the Holy Spirit with it."[4] Two hundred years later, the wind of the Holy Spirit used those very words of Luther to breathe upon the heart of another great reformer, John Wesley, who was not un-similar to Nicodemus. As a very devout preacher and teacher, he traveled overseas as a missionary minister, but a great emptiness gnawed at him inside.

According to his journal, he worked in ministry more than ten years before he experienced the inner assurance that he truly did belong to God. He moved from a mere form of religion to an intimate relationship with the Savior, Jesus Christ. He wrote, "… Even though I believed, I had not been renewed in the image of God. I had no communion with God so that I could dwell in Him, and He in me."[5] When he died, he left behind his Bible, his saddle, and the Methodist Church.

One hundred years after Wesley, a young man with only a fifth-grade education impacted the world as never before. Evangelist Dwight L. Moody said, "I was born of the flesh in 1837. I was born of the Spirit in 1856. That which is born of the flesh will die. That which is born of the Spirit will live forever."[6]

And that's the way the faith has been passed down for more than 2,000 years—one heart at a time.

When you arrive at home plate, the only call that will count will come from the Father who will simply ask, "Did you come by way of first base? By way of My Son?"

You must be born again. Because you can never gain ground as a Christian until you are one.

---

[1] Rev. Ted Baker, "The Parable of the Christian Life," Mafair United Methodist Church, July 1985.

[2] Paul Little, *How To Give Away Your Faith*, Inter-Varsity Press, 1966, 25–27.

[3] David Seamands, *Healing for Damaged Emotions,* Victor Books, 1981, 69.

[4] Dr. Robert G. Tuttle, Jr. *John Wesley: His Life and Theology,* Francis Asbury Press of Zondervan Publishing House, 1978, 193.

[5] Tuttle 193–194.

[6] A.P. Fitt, *The Shorter Life of D.L. Moody*, Moody Press, 1900, 5.

# CHAPTER 3

# FOLLOWING HARD AFTER HIM
### *"The Burning Heart"*

*Jesus said, 'Love the Lord your God with all your passion ...'*
*This is the most important, the first on any list.*
**MATTHEW 22:37** MSG

O ur youngest son had a passion for playing basketball, and every week his coach sent home an exercise chart that required discipline and hard work. At the bottom of the sheet, the coach always signed off saying "You gotta love the game!"

The coach knew that passion for the game was essential, not optional. He knew that when his players got tired or lazy or had something else they would rather be doing, it would be passion that would keep them on track.

Love of the game causes people to expend large amounts of time and money with no hesitation at all. They will sit in cold rain for hours watching two teams battle over a piece of pigskin. College students will camp out all night on campus lawns to get tickets for a basketball game. Some will even make radical adjustments to their plans, like scheduling the birth of a baby so it will not interfere with tournament season.

## FOLLOWING HARD

What does it mean if you said that you cheered hard for your team or that your team played hard in a game? Or that you ran hard in a track event or played hard in a tennis match? What would it mean if you worked hard to clean your car or your room or write an essay? It would mean that you gave it your all, that you held nothing back, that no inconvenience or discomfort made you quit, and that you spared no effort.

I recall driving a van full of middle-school boys to a sporting event out of town. I could not believe the degree to which they could recall minute sports facts, remote statistics, and even specific plays that had occurred years before! Because they loved the game, they had an insatiable appetite for sports information.

The psalmist says, "My soul followeth hard after thee" (Psalm 63:8 KJV). In the same way that those boys were intense about their sports knowledge, so we are to be intense about following hard after our God.

## THE POWER OF APPETITES

Jesus knew that our appetites are powerful, driving forces that will determine what we pursue and how we spend our time. In the same way that hunger and appetite are characteristics of a newborn baby, the distinguishing characteristic of the person newly born again of God is a hunger to know God. "The mark of one who walks in the Spirit is that he has an insatiable appetite for Jesus."[1]

It is the very nature of life to want to grow. Young children always want to be bigger. They are not content to remain small, helpless and dependent. And for sure, none of us want to be told that you are too young to do anything.

Likewise, you now have a newly born spirit. Therefore, do not be content to remain in the infant stage, but "… long to grow up into the fullness of your salvation; cry for this as a baby cries for his milk" (1 Peter 2:3 TLB). The verb "long to" is the same as our word for "crave" or "desire," which means to have an eager and intense desire—a passion for something.

If a newborn child lacks appetite, it is considered to be a significant problem and a threat to their well-being. In the same way, our level of hunger and passion for God is an indicator of spiritual health. "Acute desire must be present or their will be no manifestation of Christ."[2] The spirit born from above will hunger for God's Word and time with Him in prayer. Since Christ's spirit in you can only feed on things from above, it will shrivel and be malnourished if it is not fed spiritual food. The world around you will not suffice.

## APPETITES ARE DAILY

Life is so daily, isn't it? Have you noticed that? If you want to diet effectively, you must diet daily. If you want to increase endurance through running, exercise or weight lifting, you must do it daily. You wouldn't consider yourself to be a jogger if you only ran once a week, or a ballplayer if you only practiced every now and then. If we are not doing something *daily*, the chances are we really aren't doing it well at all.

Physical appetites are also quite daily. Regardless of how much we may consume in a given day, the next day we are hungry again. Knowing this, the person who desires to be found in Christ must grant Him access to their daily life. You cannot get to know Jesus with a hit-or-miss, once-a-week-on-Sunday approach. You have to go beyond being interested in Him to placing your daily identity in Him.

## SEDUCED BY THE SECONDARY

Jesus taught that multitudes of people deny God access to their daily lives. "There was once man who threw a great dinner party and invited many. When it was time for dinner, he sent out his servant to the invited guests, saying, 'Come on in; the food's on the table.' Then they all began to beg off, one after another, making excuses. The first said, 'I bought a piece of property and need to look it over. Send my regrets.' Another said, 'I just bought five teams of oxen, and I really need to check them out. Send my regrets.' And yet another said, 'I just got married and need to get home to my wife'" (Luke 14:16–20 MSG).

This parable illustrates the snare of the secondary. Note that it is not "bad" things that kept the people from coming. It was actually the good things in life that crowded out the "God things." Caught up in the pursuit of earthly matters, sitting down to feast with the Father gets squeezed out. "Busy, preoccupied people never get to know Christ."[3]

The real problem wasn't the cattle, the wife, or the land. These people lacked a daily appetite for fellowship with their God.

It is interesting that God doesn't have any commentary about the various reasons the guests gave for not coming to the banquet. That is because God sees things differently than we do. While we like to analyze the various reasons why the people did not attend, from God's viewpoint there are only two kinds of people: Those who come, and those who don't.

To Jesus, one reason is no more acceptable than another for turning down the Father's invitation. The people were too busy with their own agenda to recognize that they were refusing God Himself. They were *interested* in the Father's banquet but with a "catch me later" mentality. Every day your heavenly Father awaits your arrival expectantly, longing for your company, and hoping you want His. But too often we Christians are just too busy. "Love ya, Lord, but I can't stay ... got things to do ..."

I am sure you know countless Christians who live this way. You may be doing this yourself. At some time you received Jesus into your heart, but you've not allowed Him to grow up in you. You want to "be with Jesus" when you die, but you're too busy to be interested in Him here. Would you really know Him? There are no tourists in heaven. Only children at home.

Loving God with all your heart, soul, mind, and strength does not allow for half-measures. Jesus knows that your passion and hunger will drive you to Him every time because nothing else will satisfy. He desires access to your daily life. The first and greatest commandment essentially means, "Ya gotta love Me! You gotta desire Me, crave Me above all else! Do not be seduced by secondary pursuits."

Jesus warns that the cares of the world and the deceitfulness of riches will choke out the life of the Spirit in your life. One dictionary defines the word "identity" as "the collective aspects by which a person is definitely recognized or known." Is your identity in Him? Are you known as His? Do you wear His team jersey? If so, you will have a spiritual hunger for Him alone that nothing else can satisfy.

## WHERE HUNGER TAKES YOU

There is a reason why hunger for God is so important. Just as your busyness will keep you from knowing who God is, your hunger for God will take you straight to the place of getting to know Him personally where your desires will begin to change. Because the presence of God changes everything.

## A STORY

Our family had a close friend who was raised in a Christian home and baptized at eight years of age as a symbol of his new birth in Christ. Yet as he grew into a popular teen, he only appeared to be a Christian. He began to sneak out at night for fun with alcohol, petty theft, and vandalism. I knew of the parents' heartache as they anguished over what to do. They tried everything from harsh punishments, severe rules, tapping the phone line, even weekly counseling sessions, but nothing changed.

Though this young man had been born again, he had not regularly fed his new nature. Thus other appetites began to take over. His appetites for adventure, curiosity, sensual gratification, and even rebellion grew daily, while his spiritual appetite shrunk to the point that it no longer had an influence over him. One morning at 2 a.m., the parents got a call from the police. This was the last straw.

Out of desperation, they decided to try a different approach. In addition to some corrective measures, they made the decision to send him to a Christian camp whose purpose is to introduce young people to the person of Jesus Christ. It was a risk. He could abuse the privilege, waste the money, and use the opportunity to get into more trouble! This bold decision took courage and faith. Yet these parents could do this because they personally knew the Lord themselves.

Despite her hopes, the mother somewhat dreaded his return. She wasn't sure she was strong enough to handle him at home again. It was after midnight when the bus pulled into the parking lot of a shopping center. She turned and saw him standing by the car. The moment she saw him, she knew by his countenance that he was changed. He was radiant. He had reconnected with the Jesus he once loved, and the presence of Jesus had altered everything about his life!

One young man has said it this way, "If I really believe that God is present in my life that does more to deal with the problem of sin than trying to deal with the problem of sin."[4]

## TAKE IT TO THE NEXT LEVEL

Being in God's presence takes you to a new level! Just as pesky insects, gnats, mosquitoes, flies, and mice cannot survive high altitudes, so your lower appetites *will not* survive the altitude of God's greatness. Once exposed to the purity of who God is, that language, those pictures, that alcohol and theft no longer have an appeal. As the song, "Turn Your Eyes upon Jesus," says: "And the things of earth will grow strangely dim in the light of His glory and grace."

All our appetites are God-given. He filled the Garden of Eden with every pleasure imaginable! We are meant to enjoy beauty, the sexual relationship, intimacy, sleep, food, and pleasure. But when these healthy appetites get out of balance, or take perverted turns, they become unhealthy distortions of God's original plan.

Believe me, the most effective antidote to temptation is to simply draw closer to God! Instead of striving so hard to battle issues out of your own knowledge, dependent on your own strength of will, kick your life into a higher gear by adding more of Jesus. This will increase your appetite, and one day you will quietly realize that your lower appetites are disappearing, falling away with no effort on your part. You have found something far better to feed on. Your desires have been changed by His presence.

## Truth is...

**The most effective antidote to temptation is to simply draw closer to God.**

Think about those people at the mall who stand outside their eateries to offer samples of their food on toothpicks. They are counting on their sample and your appetite to bring you into their restaurant. In the same way, once you truly taste the things of the Lord, no substitute will ever satisfy again. When you have had a delicious steak at a fine restaurant, you don't have any desire to stop on the way home at a cheap drive-in to eat a rubbery burger. Why? Because you are satisfied. You have had the best.

You may have "tasted church" or "tasted religion" or "tasted duty" and found these to be dry and stale. But when you taste the richest of foods—the honey from the rock that satisfies, the bread of life and the sparkling living water that is Jesus Christ—then you can say with the psalmist, "Taste and see that the LORD is good"(Psalm 34:8).

This is what happened to our friend. Fellowship with Jesus changed his tastes, appetites and desires. Four years later, he continued to be one of two high school students who prayed daily at the flag pole of their school every morning at 7 a.m. Today he is a loving husband and father of two, glad that he returned to his Lord.

## "BUT I KNOW SOMEONE WHO ..."

Do you know someone who has fallen away and not returned to God? Yes, so do I. Plenty of Christians fall away, not just in terms of their morality, but in losing their passion for God. As a result, they return to their old patterns and habits.

Special faces come to my mind. Faces that used to have bright eyes and young people with tender hearts for God. Faces of sixth graders who "couldn't wait" to organize their first "See You at the Pole" event for the National Day of Prayer. Faces that have made banners that still hang high in our youth room at church, faces that have sung "better is one day in your courts than thousands elsewhere" with powerful conviction and hands pointed as high as their arms could reach.

Now the passion is gone. Seduced by the world, they stopped coming to the banquet. What is to be said?

If their faith was only conformity faith, or indoctrination faith, instead of saving faith, as discussed in chapter two, they have not been redeemed by the Lamb or re-born of the Spirit.

## Get Real:

When you have just had a delicious steak, why would you stop at a cheap drive-in for a rubbery hamburger?

But if they truly gave their lives to Christ, and are born again from above, they will return. There is no way they cannot. Jesus says, "No one can snatch them away from me, for my Father has given them to me, and he is more powerful than anyone else" (John 10:28–29 NLT ).

As I write this, I have great joy for one who has recently returned to making the Lord the first love of her life. Those who do not return remain discontent, empty, impoverished. If they return to the Lord only at death, they will still be received. But they will have forfeited the life

God had intended for them to have *here*, the hunk of history they could have shaped for Him here.

## HIS PRESENCE EQUALS PRIME TIME

Satan knows the awesome truth that encountering the living presence of Jesus Christ will alter everything. That is why he will do all he can to keep you away from "the banquet." He knows that keeping you away will render you powerless. Thus one of your greatest struggles will become how to spend your time. Satan wants to increase your appetites for anything that will keep you away from God. He knows exactly where the daily battle is won or lost.

Today the competition for our time keeps us from attending youth group, Bible studies, Christian camps, and retreats that provide uninterrupted time alone with God—and it is crushing us. Without God's daily presence none of us can grow up into the fullness of our salvation. Our lives require the fellowship that only He can provide. We need His truth, His biblical worldview, wisdom, and discernment to cope with the pressing demands of daily life.

## INTIMACY

Human beings have a great need for intimacy. I'm not speaking here of sexual intimacy, though that is where many turn to meet their needs for intimacy. What I'm speaking of is when a person knows you through and through and still loves you anyway! In fact, your closeness to another person will be in direct proportion to how honest you are with that person—there can't be any facades or superficiality if you want to experience true fellowship with another person.

The result of your hunger for God will be a quality of intimacy like none other. Many have expressed this feeling: "I always lived in fear that if people really knew me, they wouldn't like me. And my goal in relationships was to keep people just distant enough that they would only see the good stuff. It never occurred to me that the God who knows all of me could really like me—that He would want an intimate relationship with me." What God wants most from you is not maturity or sinlessness. What God wants is you. Christianity is a love affair, a relationship. It's all about being found and being secure in Him.

## ANOTHER YOUNG MAN

Another young man I knew had great difficulty in school, struggled with academics, attention deficit disorder, and failed a grade. In many ways, he was a misfit. But one thing Aaron had going for him was a genuine appetite for God that compelled him to come to the banquet.

One time, after attending a youth event where we all experienced the presence of God, Aaron came to Bible study. He shared that because God had spoken to him he had decided to take down all the heavy metal posters from his walls, give away his CDs, and to stop wearing black all the time. As amazing as this change was for him, the most amazing thing that occurred was observing the other young people in the group. I watched as those very sophisticated, successful youth were reduced to tears when they saw Aaron's heart for God. He loved his God. His new identity with God's purity gave them a taste of honey from the rock, and they yearned for more. People today still remember how totally Aaron changed. His hunger has carried him a long way.

A life with no regrets. I have never known of anyone who truly belongs to Jesus who has ever regretted coming to the banquet.

The psalmist boldly said of his relationship with God: "For you are with me" (Psalm 23:4). He understood that it was God who would meet his needs, find Him when he was lost, feed him when he was hungry, fight for him when he was in trouble, and tenderly care for his wounds in the same way the shepherd cared for his sheep. No wonder he proclaimed, "Bless the LORD, O my soul: and all that is within me, bless his holy name" (Psalm 103:1 KJV). He loved God with all that he had within him, heart, mind, soul and strength.

## THE BURNING HEART

The first fellowship of the burning heart comes from the Gospel of Luke when some disciples, in great despair, were returning to their homes after the crucifixion of Jesus. A stranger, unrecognizable to them, joined them on their journey. When their eyes were opened and they realized it was Jesus, they said to one another, "Were not our hearts burning within us when he talked with us on the road and opened the Scriptures to us?" (Luke 24:32).

The heart became a part of the personal seal of the great reformer, John Calvin (circa 1536), which showed a hand offering a heart to God. When John Wesley had an encounter with the presence of Jesus on May 24, 1738, he wrote, "I felt my heart strangely warmed."[5] From that moment nothing ever deterred him from a fully abandoned life.

In 1947, a tiny lady in Hollywood, California, Henrietta Mears, loved big hats and young people. She, too, identified herself as belonging to "the fellowship of the burning heart." As a result, one of the young people her life impacted was a man named Billy Graham. By his own words, the turning point of his life occurred at Miss Mears' Forest Home Christian Camp when he was thirty-one. Can you begin to fathom how many lives have been brought to Christ through this one man alone? Furthermore, isn't it astounding that all of those people were indirectly birthed from the burning heart of one tiny woman with funny hats?[6]

A.W. Tozer, called "a 20th century prophet even in his lifetime, delighted that his identity was found in the "fellowship of the burning heart" because "his walk with God was a priority with him and he allowed nothing to interfere."[7]

So keep it going! Keep your heart on fire and offer it to God. It makes a lot of sense. After all, John the Baptist said, "I baptize you with water for repentance. But after me will come one who ... will baptize you with the Holy Spirit and with fire." (Matthew 3:11).

Spoilt for everything but Him. And no regrets on the part of any person mentioned above.

Let nothing interfere.

---

[1] David Wilkerson, *Hungry for More of Jesus*, Fleming Revell, 1992, 105.

[2] A.W. Tozer, *The Pursuit of God*, Christian Publications, l982, 17.

[3] Wilkerson, 67.

[4] Mike Yaconelli, National Youth Workers Convention, October 1993.

[5] Dr. Robert Tuttle, Jr., *John Wesley: His Life and Theology*, Francis Asbury Press of Zondervan Publishing, l978, 195.

[6] Earl O. Roe, editor, *Dream Big: The Henrietta Mears Story*, Regal Books, 269–270, 282, 295, 336.

[7] Tozer, 1.

# CHAPTER 4

# LONGING FOR GOD'S TRUTH
## *"The Teachable Heart"*

*I long for your instructions more than I can tell.*
**PSALM 119:20** TLB

**W**hen I was a new Christian at age eighteen, this verse from the psalmist really grabbed me. Since then I, too, have always longed for God's Word. I learned early on, however, that I was part of a small minority.

So you can imagine how excited I became when chaperoning a youth trip to discover that one of the girls in my room read her Bible every night and actually highlighted passages. (I can still visualize those aqua lines today.) She did not do this to show off or to perform a nightly ritual. She showed me a verse that was helping her. She was only in the eighth grade yet learning to find her identity in Christ.

The psalmist had an intensely teachable heart. He wanted to know God's thoughts. You can hear the earnestness in his voice: "I am but a pilgrim here on earth: how I need a map—and your commands are my chart and guide. I long for your instructions more than I can tell" (Psalm 119:19–20 TLB).

"The Bible is the mind of God on a printed page. We are told to cling to it, believe it, hold fast to it and never depart from it. Man would not have written this book if he could because it reveals the sin of man and provides only one solution, His redeeming love on the cross. Man couldn't have written it if he wanted to and he wouldn't have written it if he could have."[1]

The one who truly desires to know Him will long for God's Word. Twenty-four times in Psalm 119, the writer refers to God's Word as his "delight" that he loves "with all my heart." It is not to be a dusty book on a bottom shelf. Neither is it a religious book about how to act. Only God's Word will satisfy the one who belongs to Him. It is life itself.

It is the only book you'll ever read that is eternal and where the author Himself is fully present with you. It has survived every kind of criticism, attack and opposition imaginable, being burned and cut into shreds. While those who burned it are gone, today there are more translations and copies than ever available all over the world. "The grass withers and the flowers fall, but the word of our God stands forever" (Isaiah 40:8).

It is the bread of God to feed you, living water that springs up to give new life, the milk and meat to nourish and grow you. It is more valuable than the finest gold, more precious than rubies. It is the tree of life, sweeter than the honeycomb, and nothing you desire can measure up to God's Word. It alone is an inexhaustible supply of wisdom, guidance, correction and training, a spring and fountain that never runs dry. Supremely, it is the revelation of the life, teachings, death, and resurrection of Jesus Christ. Its truth is the standard by which all things will be measured, and it will last forever.

"God is real, and He has spoken. And He is the measure of all things—not man."[2]

## DO YOU HAVE AQUA LINES?

Knowing this, "we cheat ourselves when we do not access every book, every truth, every verse and every page of our Bibles for the promises and commands God has for us."[3]

What is your relationship with this most precious, priceless book? Do you have colored lines with dates beside them to record when God taught you a specific truth as did my eighth-grade friend? It is imperative for the Christian to feed the newly born spirit lest it shrivel and become mute and you will find that the world will "squeeze you into its own mould" (Romans 12:2 PHILLIPS).

It doesn't take long to recognize that this is radical paradigm shift. "'For my thoughts are not your thoughts, neither are your ways my ways,' declares the LORD. 'As the heavens are higher than the earth, so are my ways higher than your ways and my thoughts than your thoughts'" (Isaiah 55:8–9).

As you learn to know God, you'll be astounded to see how far out of alignment our human ways are with His. Gradually you'll begin to understand that you can't believe any way you want to and belong to Him. You cannot live any way you want to and love God with all your heart.

You'll come to understand that learning His Word is the only thing that can transform the way you think. It will rattle the status quo. Where else would you learn that we must die in order to live, lose your life to save it, give in order to receive, be last if you want to be first, become a servant in order to be great, and live for Him if you want to accomplish anything that will last forever?

## WHAT IS YOUR MEASURE?

"The Bible is not subject to you; you are subject to it."[4] If you make God's Word subject to you, God has been removed from His rightful place. This is comparable to tuning your piano to another piano instead of to the tuning fork. Your life may be in tune with that of another person, yet both of you will be out of tune with the standard.

When you don't believe that God alone gives us words of truth, your life will be based on what you think. Since the majority of people live this way, everyone's "I think" must hold equal weight. Therefore nothing can be considered absolute or certain.

This is illustrated in an amusing commercial where a grandfather, who was a professional basketball player, is talking to his grandson about how the sport had changed over the years. The punch line is that he kept up well with all the changes in the game "until they put in those movable goals."

Truth that is constantly changing would make it impossible to know God. The Scripture says He does not change: "Jesus Christ is the same yesterday and today and forever" (Hebrews 13:8). Only God's truth remains fixed, trustworthy and utterly reliable. You can be secure in the certainty that His goals are immovable. His truth is unchanging whether you live in the first or the thirty-first century.

## STANDARDS WE RESPECT

As a spectator of numerous sports, I have come to an astonishing conclusion. It's not the thrill of touchdown, an awesome home run, or the three-point basket that produces white knuckles, nail-biting, and yelling. What really creates the awesome suspense, thrills, and energy in an athletic competition is the presence of a standard.

It's the boundaries, the perimeters that generate all that excitement. Will the three-point shot go in before the buzzer ends the game? Will the power hit in baseball be a home run or merely a foul tip? Will his foot be inside the boundary line for that touchdown pass?

Standards define how an athlete must play the game. Consider the confusion if each team came to the NCAA basketball tournament with their own set of rules. The only way different teams can compete is because they all consent to play by the established regulation standards of the sport. Thus the challenge is to see who can succeed the best within the same given boundaries. Without finish lines, perimeters, time clocks and regulation play, there would be no sport, no thrill and no challenge because no one could ever win.

## THE PURPOSE OF A STANDARD

Consider the disorder if the fans were allowed to call the shots. For instance, in football, the team with the ball has four attempts to advance ten yards down field. If they fail, they lose possession of the ball. Thus, the fourth try is always intense. Picture the scene: They run the play, but it isn't clear if the team got the yards for the first down. Is it first and ten or fourth and inches? The whole game could depend on this one call. People in the stands are yelling, "He's got it!" and on the other side of the field they're yelling, "No way!" Fans can become livid when officials make a call they don't like.

Do the referees ask anyone what he "thinks"? Or do they poll the crowd for a majority consensus? No, they don't say a word. They simply get "the chain." This is merely two poles connected by a chain that is exactly ten yards long. This standard length never changes. Despite all the yelling, the referees decide based on the length of that chain. It is a fixed standard. Without the measuring device of the chain, there would be complete chaos.

The standard is not subject to the crowd's desire nor can each team bring their "own" chain. No matter how advanced our technology becomes, no matter how intelligent and sophisticated the human race becomes, ten yards will always be ten yards. This means that the crowd must submit to the truth the standard reveals.

The worst incidents of fighting and yelling between our boys always occurred when they played "sandlot" ball games with no referee. Each one was sure he was right and tried to call the game according to the way he saw it. These disputes would carry over to the supper table, the nightly shower, and even to bedtime. Countless people live with this kind of dissension and strife every day of their lives. Yet God's Word says, "Let the peace of Christ rule in your hearts ... you are called to live in harmony" (Colossians 3:15 PHILLIPS). The Greek word here for "rule" means to "act as an umpire." His "rule" over my life will produce peace.

This means we must allow Him, not ourselves, to make the calls in our lives—because, like the ten-yard chain in football, He is the standard.

## WHAT DOES THIS HAVE TO DO WITH ME?

Since God's Word provides the guidance we need, what could possibly be more important than to learn what He has to say?

Clearly it is our lives—not footballs and pianos—that are in the greatest need of reliable truth. Wouldn't it be unreasonable to think that the God, who created you to have a relationship with Him, would not provide a way for you to get to know Him? While we readily embrace the physical standards that bring meaning and order to our lives, we can be quick to reject the spiritual standards God has placed in His Word to bring the same order and purpose.

"How can a young man stay pure? By reading your Word and following its rules. I have tried my best to find you—don't let me wander off from your instructions" (Psalm 119:9–10 TLB).

## STANDARDS WE RESIST

How teachable is your heart?

The prevailing mind-set that has saturated our society today is epitomized by the phrase "whatever." It goes like this:

"Whatever you're into is okay": pluralism

"Whatever you believe is okay": relativism

"Whatever you believe, keep it to yourself": privatization

But God has spoken, and He has not said "whatever"! All things are not the same to Him. Jesus exposed Satan as the father of lies: "There is no truth in him ... he is a liar and the father of lies" (John 8:44). "The lies are impeccably factual. They contain no errors ... But they are lies all the same because they claim to tell us who we are and omit everything about our origin in God and our destiny in God."[5]

Jesus also said that the vast majority of people trust in their personal judgment as the standard for life and will not uphold solid biblical truth. Only the teachable few sit at His feet to learn of Him. When you know God, you want to live by a standard that is higher than what is legal, socially acceptable, or would be allowed by your family or church. For the Christian, God is the measure of that latest date, movie, music, party, attitude, viewpoint, or habit.

## WHAT DID JESUS DO?

Jesus launched His ministry by reading from the book of Isaiah and stated profoundly that He was the fulfillment of every word Isaiah had prophesied. (See Luke 4:16–21.)

For forty days in the wilderness, Jesus battled the temptations from Satan and not once did He say "I think." He had his own aqua lines and dealt with Satan by saying, "It is *written* ..." (See Matthew 4:1–11.) He did not dispute "a single dot or comma" (Matthew 5:18 PHILLIPS) of God's recorded Word, which was then the Old Testament. Scripture was infallible to Jesus and it was His authority. For you to be found in Him, can you do any less?

### Truth is...

God has spoken to us in His Word, and He has not said *"whatever."*

## THE EFFECT OF HIS WORD

Paul wrote the words of 2 Timothy 3:16–17 to a young church leader named Timothy, reminding him of how Scripture was written and how useful it is in our lives: "All Scripture is God-breathed and is useful for teaching, rebuking, correcting and training in righteousness, so that the man [person] of God may be thoroughly equipped for every good work."

**"All scripture is God-breathed."** Not just some parts, but *all* of it is "God-breathed"—"all Scripture." Whether or not you believe this is the most significant and crucial decision you will ever make as a Christian.

It's a tough stand to take because it is decisive. Many will view you as a fanatic. I used to think that way myself! Some will consider you to be uneducated, ignorant, judgmental, and naïve. But that's okay when you know the One who is Truth. It has been written through men but was given by the inspiration of God. I'll be a fanatic for God any day over the secondary options. Aqua lines for me.

You see, the person without the Spirit of God finds the things of God foolish. This means you can never convince another person that God's Word is true only by debating the point. Only the Holy Spirit can bring a person from darkness to the light. Only then does an insatiable appetite for the Word set in.

A.W. Tozer, a man called "a 20th century prophet," wrote, "I am a Bible Christian and if an archangel with a wingspread as broad as a constellation shining like the sun

**Truth is...**

What you believe about God's Word is the single most critical and significant decision you will ever make as a Christian.

were to come and offer me some new truth, I'd ask him for a reference. If he could not show me where it is found in the Bible, I would bow him out and say, 'I'm awfully sorry, you don't bring any references with you.'"[6]

Let's look at some of the ways God's Word can (and should) affect us.

**"Useful."** The word "profitable" in the King James Version of 2 Timothy 3:16–17 is translated as "useful" in many newer versions. When something works, it sells like crazy. We're all about what works. We're also all about what will profit us. Did you know that one of the most discussed topics in the Bible is money? Other practical (useful or profitable) topics in the Bible are fear, worry, despair, sexual pleasure, marriage, hope and love.

God's Word helped me find my way through the maze of dating and marriage, how to raise my sons, how to tame my tongue, how to understand my purpose, and how to know Him as more real than the world around me. It is infinitely more useful than my computer, which can crash or contract a virus, or any self-help book. My Bible is currently unglued from the binding and literally in shreds of all colors.

**"For showing us truth"** (MSG). Are His instructions clear to you? The psalmist says "the unfolding of your words gives light" (Psalm 119:130). It sheds light on any situation you will ever face, bringing wisdom and discernment.

The future holds many challenges regarding morality and ethics. We are not far away from medical technology that would allow you to program a "designer baby" by selecting the gender, IQ, and abilities for your child. Would you do this? What would be the basis for your decision? Would you have wanted to be programmed this way by your parents?

The Bible is also the most honest book you can read. For example, check this out: "In the last days it is going to be very difficult to be a Christian. For people will love only themselves and their money; they will be proud and boastful ... disobedient to their parents, ungrateful to them ... and will think nothing of immorality ... They will be hotheaded, puffed up with pride, and prefer good times to worshipping God. They will go to church, yes, but they won't really believe anything they hear" (2 Timothy 3:1–5 TLB).

**"For showing people what is wrong in their lives, for correcting faults"** (NCV) is another reason God's Word is profitable to us. Did you know that God corrects those He loves? (See Hebrews 12:6.) Do you allow anyone to correct the things in your life that are wrong? God's correction is a sign that you belong to Him!

One day I was so steamed at a friend that I decided the time had come to tell her off in a nice way. But before I did, I sat down for a quiet time with God and His Word. After reading several portions of Scripture, I was feeling pretty good about everything—until I read the very last verse: "Do not let me hear of you ... being a busybody and prying into other people's affairs" (1 Peter 4:15 TLB).

Is that correction or what? Needless to say, that changed my plans for that day. And how grateful am I today? This person is still a dear friend whom God protected me from losing. When a rebuke comes from other people, especially parents, you may become defensive and ignore it. But "whoever heeds correction gains understanding" (Proverbs 15:32).

Have you ever looked back at an old photo and yelled, "Awful! Those clothes were so stupid, those glasses so horrible, my hair was the pits! Why didn't someone tell me?" The teachable heart wants to be corrected! "I have strayed like a lost sheep" (Psalm 119:176) ... "I hate every wrong path" (Psalm 119:128) ... "Let no sin rule over me" (Psalm 119:133). How might your life be different if you came before God with heart like this?

I can have a sharp tongue, a critical spirit, or a complaining attitude. But the Word of God tells me that my tongue should bring healing like a tree of life (Proverbs 15:4) and that my gentleness should be evident to all (Philippians 4:5). That "all" means my home, my family, clerks in stores, waiters in restaurants, and bus drivers. It harms those around me, especially since they see it long before I do! God rebukes these aspects of my life and once I finally get it, my first thought is always, "Why didn't I see this sooner?"

**"Training us to live God's way"** (MSG). The exercise chart my son brought home was a tool to produce physical fitness. Paul told Timothy, "Train yourself to be godly. For physical training is of some value, but godliness has value for all things ... both for the present life and the life to come" (1 Timothy 4:7–8).

Are you in training to become spiritually fit in your thoughts and actions? It takes God's Spirit to keep quiet when you are angry, to place others ahead of yourself, to return good for evil and to overlook an offense. You cannot do this without consulting His manual for instructions regarding what to do and asking His Holy Spirit to enable you to do it.

When your life is found in Him, you will yearn to know what He says. "I have thought much about your words, and stored them in my heart so that they would hold me back from sin" (Psalm 119:11 TLB).

**"In righteousness."** In Psalm 23 David says that his Shepherd leads (or guides) him "in paths of righteousness for his name's sake" (v.3). Our fallen human nature isn't naturally righteous. We must be led to put others first, return good for evil, serve food to homeless people, clean the toilets after a youth retreat, or sacrifice our time and comfort for others.

Sometimes I want to hang a "Do Not Disturb" sign over my life. Now I have learned that He makes that call, not me. "Direct me in the path of your commands, for there I find delight" (Ps.119:35) describes a teachable heart.

## GOD'S WORD WILL LAST FOREVER

You will never regret building your life on God's Word. You know all those books that end up on a 75%-off table? You'll never find the Bible there, on an overstock table, or out of print. "Long ago I learned from your statues that you established them to last forever" (Psalm 119: 152).

If it were proven one day that Confucius or Buddha never lived, their teachings would live on unaltered. If the Muslims discovered that Muhammad never lived, it would not change one thing about Islam. In contrast, however, if it were ever proven that Jesus Christ never lived, all of Christianity would crumble into a pile of dust because our faith is not built solely on the teachings of Jesus Christ. Christianity is based of the *life* that Jesus lived, the sacrificial death He died to save us, and the power of the resurrection that overcame death itself. For Christians, Truth is a person.

Now "I run in the path of your commands, for you have set my heart free" (Psalm119: 32).

---

1 Charles Stanley, "In Touch" broadcast, 2/2/2011.

2 Dr. Francis Schaeffer, 700 Club interview, 1982.

3 Henry Blackaby and Richard Blackaby, *Experiencing God Day By Day*, Broadman and Holman Publishers, 1998, 337.

4 Schaeffer.

5 Eugene Peterson, *A Long Obedience in the Same Direction*, Inter-Varsity Press, 1980, 23.

6 A.W. Tozer, Quotes

# CHAPTER 5

# WHEN I FAIL
## *"The Transformed Heart"*

*When someone becomes a Christian he becomes a brand new person inside. He is not the same anymore. A new life has begun!*
**2 CORINTHIANS 5:17** TLB

I sat in a room filled with young people who were telling me that their biggest problem in deciding to follow Jesus was fear of failure. They didn't believe they could succeed at being a Christian.

When you understand that the goal of life is likeness to Jesus, you may likely say, "Not me. You don't know me. It'll never happen." All of us know there is a huge gap between what we are and what we ought to be. Do you truly believe that the common person can become like Jesus? You know how weak you are and don't trust yourself. Truth is, no matter how strong you are or how committed, you cannot make yourself into a disciple.

But I have good news.

## LOW AIM

James Russell Lowell has said, "It is not failure but low aim that is the great crime."[1] Trusting God for too little, not asking Him for great things is therefore one of our greatest crimes. You are surrounded by Christians who are content with mediocrity in their spiritual lives. The common excuse for having low aim is. "I'm only human." People who believe this will live a life limited by their own ways of thinking. They remain in their comfort zone, undertaking only what they know they can handle in their own strength. But the comfort zone is not nearly what it is cracked up to be. It easily becomes predictable, monotonous and dull.

If you are willing to move through your fears to seek what God has promised us, your life will be used by God to accomplish more than you could ever imagine or think. [2]

## THEY SAID IT COULDN'T BE DONE

For centuries, man dreamed of breaking the four-minute mile, but no one believed it was possible. But in 1954, an Englishman, Roger Bannister, did indeed break four minutes. Suddenly, within the hearts of runners across all continents surged the belief, "I bet I could do that!" In rapid succession, athletes everywhere began to run the mile, not only in four minutes, but in even less time, because they had seen it could be done.

The life of the disciple Simon Peter shows us the reality of how our lives can also go far beyond what we could ever imagine or think. He is our "Roger Bannister" because he shows us how a common person can become a disciple and be re-made into the likeness of Jesus.

## SIMON: SHIFTING SAND

He was not at all the kind of person you would choose to be a disciple. He was a rough man who lived an uneducated, dull life. Neither refined nor cultured, he was a crude fisherman, a blustering kind of guy whose volcanic temperament could burst into profanity at any moment. When he tried to do the right thing, he failed again and again. He was not good religious material. What did he have to offer Jesus?

Yet this is exactly who Jesus called to follow Him. And with no hesitation, no excuses of any kind, Simon beached his boat and left all to follow the Lord.

## THE MAKING OF A DISCIPLE

Like Simon, when you come to Jesus, you come just as you are, no matter what. If you are snobby or shy, lazy or compulsive before becoming a Christian, you will likely have those same qualities the next day. But once you're His, every part of your life begins to change. You begin to see aspects of your life that you never saw before and realize they do not line up with Jesus. Now you have a new desire to depart from self and serve Him.

When I went off to college as a brand new Christian, I was filled with weaknesses. I was focused primarily on myself and lacked discipline. I knew only a little about God's Word and didn't think about the needs of others. But because my heart was spoken for, I had a new appetite to know God. "Disciple" means "learner," "one who learns from another." That meant I had a new priority for my life.

In the beginning, the only thing about Simon that changed was his direction. He dropped his nets and followed Jesus. But that was enough because Jesus said, "Come with me. I'll make a new kind of fisherman out of you" (Matthew 4:19 MSG). Jesus assumed the responsibility for transforming this unrefined fisherman.

## DO THESE SOUND FAMILIAR?

After Simon left the beach to follow Jesus, he was:

**Inconsiderate.** Once he invited several men to his house despite the fact that his mother-in-law was sick in bed. We can imagine how she felt about having a group of smelly, famished fisherman come to her home looking for a good meal! Yet Jesus used this opportunity to draw attention to the woman's need by performing a miracle of healing. Once cured, she rose to "wait on them" (Matthew 8:14–15).

**Overly Self-Confident.** One night during a storm at sea, Jesus walked across the water to his frightened disciples. When Simon saw this miracle, he wanted to do the same thing! When Jesus bid him come, he immediately stepped out onto the water. In an amazing display of trust and courage, he walked several steps! But when Simon noticed the height of the waves, his rush of confidence quickly folded into fear and he began to sink. His zeal was swamped by doubt (Matthew 14:22–31).

Did he step out in faith or self-confidence? In the beginning, Simon was like shifting sand, inconsistent and unstable. But when he began to sink, this weak disciple knew where to turn for help. Immediately he cried out, "Lord, save me!" and the reaching hand of Jesus was there to save him from himself.

When life pulls you under, gasping for breath, the answers will not be found "within yourself," as so many claim. Jesus told Peter, "*I will make you*" (Matthew 4:19), not "Follow Me and read self-help books."

**Full of Human Zeal**. Simon had a lot more mouth than character. Know anyone like that? During a sacred moment when Jesus was transfigured on a mountaintop, Simon could not stop talking. Even though he had no idea what to say, he tried to take charge. When Moses and Elijah appeared from heaven, Peter wanted to build shelters for Jesus, Moses, and Elijah to live there. Even in the presence of Jesus, he wanted to lead the whole group! He was blabbering so much that it took a cloud cover to hush him up! (Matthew 17:1–8).

At this point, you might expect Jesus to send Simon away, concluding that his training as a disciple had failed. But instead, Jesus touched him and said, "Get up ... don't be afraid" (Matthew 17:7). Jesus had no intention of giving up on this man.

**Self-Interest**. It's astonishing how honest the Bible is about human nature. It records that Simon said to Jesus: "We have left all we had to follow you!" (Luke 18:28). In other words: "So now, what will we get out of it?" Aren't you glad that he asked the same question that often goes through your own minds? Jesus replied, "You won't regret it. No one who has sacrificed ... will lose out. It will all come back multiplied many times over in your lifetime. And then the bonus of eternal life!" (Luke 18:29 MSG).

**Confident in His Own Judgment**. Simon placed great value in his own opinions. He was so sure that his way of thinking was right that twice he corrected Jesus. He told Jesus that he would not have to suffer and die (Matthew 16: 22). Because he saw as man sees, he didn't understand that God's ways might involve suffering. Self-confidence was one of Simon's most dominant characteristics. When Jesus predicted that all the disciples would deny Him, Simon boasted that he would never deny the Lord (Matthew 26:31–35). He was so sure of himself that he actually argued with Jesus.

**Truth is...**

**When life pulls you under, gasping for breath, the answers will not be found 'within yourself.'**

**Divine Insight**. However, this blundering, uneducated fisherman was the first disciple to receive divine revelation from God that Jesus was indeed the Messiah. With no hesitation he boldly declared, "You are the Christ, the Son of the living God" (Matthew 16:16). For this, Jesus declared him blessed (fortunate), one to be envied, because this truth could only be revealed by the Father. It was here that Jesus gave Simon the new name Peter, "Petra," meaning rock.

**Filled with Pride**. The evening before the crucifixion, all the disciples gathered together with Jesus in the Upper Room. For three years they had eaten with Him, slept with Him, listened to Him teach, and watched Him heal the sick. Now they were arguing over which of them was the greatest. Jesus took a cloth and a basin of water to wash the feet of His followers. This act by Jesus redefined what a successful human being looks like. Greatness means becoming a servant.

"In our culture today, the notion of rank is all important. It is like a pyramid with everyone scrambling to get to the top, the apex. But in the kingdom of God, the pyramid is reversed. Jesus, the Son of Man lies at the bottom of the inverted apex. Those who would be ranked highly in His kingdom must be willing to descend, to be humbled, and even abased. If you want to be near Him that is where you must go for that is where He resides."[3]

But the prideful Peter resisted: "No way are you going to wash my feet!" (See John 13:8.) He did not want to receive such a humble act from Jesus. When Jesus stated that this cleansing was essential to become a part of His kingdom, Peter still created a fuss. He jumped up exclaiming, "Then, Lord, not just my feet but my hands and my head as well!" (See John 13:9.) He had trouble just doing what he was told! He still liked to call the shots. Humility and humbleness then, as well as today, do not come easy to the followers of Jesus.

**Inconsistent**. Although he boasted of his loyalty and strength, we see that in the Garden of Gethsemane Peter was sleeping instead of praying. When it was time to be active, he was passive (Matthew 26:40). The most zealous disciple, who said he would never forsake his Lord, could not stay awake. His human zeal had run out.

But he didn't get to sleep for long. Rudely awakened by hostile voices and the clanging of metal swords, Peter saw the temple guards who had come to arrest Jesus.

Now, it was all over. Jesus was arrested.

Suddenly Peter plunged into action and tried once more to take charge: "Then Simon Peter, who had a sword, drew it and struck the high priest's servant, cutting off his right ear" (John 18:10). He automatically rushed in to do what "seemed right" in his own eyes.

For three years he had heard Jesus instruct him to love his enemies, to turn the other cheek, to forgive those who persecute you. He had seen Jesus with the towel and the basin, washing his feet. Didn't he learn anything? Now that it was the time to be passive, he became active. And while he sliced off an ear, it is much more likely that Peter was going for the head! We certainly identify with his anger and his loving desire to protect Jesus. Yet human reasoning was still directing his life.

**Unreliable: The Greatest Failure Ever.** One final time, Peter "shifted" like sand. This confident "leader of the pack" denied Jesus. Not once, twice, but three times—just as Jesus had predicted. He could not even stand up under the questioning of a young servant girl.

As he cursed out his third denial, the rooster crowed and the guards brought Jesus back through the courtyard. Luke tells us that Jesus "turned and looked straight at Peter. Then Peter remembered the word the Lord had spoken to him" (Luke 22:61). Now he has failed beyond measure.

At that heartbreaking moment, Peter finally connected the dots and saw his sin. Though his heart truly loved Jesus, his mind continued to rely on his own judgment and ways of seeing things. And his will was weak. The confident bravado is now gone. In humility and brokenness of heart, "he went outside and wept bitterly" (Luke 22:62), collapsing in his betrayal.

Jesus is gone.

For three years, Jesus had known Peter far better than he ever knew himself. Jesus knew that under pressure, he would fold. His story is recorded in all four gospels. No one forgot or let him off the hook— except for one.

## IT DOESN'T GET ANY WORSE THAN THIS

Jesus had named Peter "the rock" upon which His church would be built. How can this be true now? No one strong as a rock would deny his Lord. We can't imagine a worse failure.

While Jesus had told his followers that He would rise from the dead, none of them believed it. No great faith can be found here. Just weak human beings reacting out of fear for their own lives. When the women came to tell the disciples that Jesus had indeed risen from the dead, "they did not believe the women, because their words seemed to them like nonsense" (Luke 24: 11). In other words, the disciples thought the women were crazy!

Peter tried his very best to be a worthy disciple but he just couldn't do it. Neither can you or I.

## NEVER CALL IT AT THE HALF

In hopeless resignation, Peter and the others returned to fishing, facing gray dawns, sandy beaches and empty nets. Again, Peter fished all night and caught nothing. Where there had been fullness, now there was nothingness.

But sportscasters know that you never call a game at the half. And remember, there was one person who knew there was more to Peter than his denial.

For in the cold, gray dawn, a stranger called from the shore, "Haven't you any fish?" When they replied "No," the stranger instructed them to throw the net on the right side of the boat to see what would happen.

"When they did, they were unable to haul the net in because of the large number of fish. Then the disciple whom Jesus loved said to Peter, 'It is the Lord!' As soon as Simon Peter heard [this] ... [he] jumped into the water. The other disciples followed in the boat, towing the net full of fish ... Jesus said to them, 'Bring some of the fish you have just caught.' Simon Peter climbed aboard and dragged the net ashore. It was full of large fish, 153, but even with so many the net was not torn."(John 21:6–11). The moment Peter recognized the Lord, he plunged into the water. He could not get to Jesus fast enough! His heart still belonged to Jesus.

There on the beach, in the streaking gold dawn, surrounded by an abundance of teeming nets, Peter now stood face to face with the risen Lord. Jesus had made no mistake when He called this man to follow Him or when He named him "the rock." Though he had failed through his human weaknesses, he was not a failure. The Lord wasn't through with His plan. Peter would still become a great fisher of men.

After a breakfast of fish, grilled over a warm fire, Jesus searched Peter's heart. Three times, one for each denial, Jesus blotted out the sin and failure. He reinstated Peter as the "rock," the leader of the little band of believers left behind, and He commissioned Peter to "feed my sheep." (See John 21:15–19.)

Jesus knows you perfectly and understands you much better than you can ever know yourself. He comprehends all of your past, and He knows all that you can do and become. You are uniquely designed to fulfill His purposes. And He can handle your weakness and failures because God says, "My power shows up best in weak people" (2 Corinthians 12:9 TLB).

## THE SECOND HALF

When Peter emerged for the second half, he was a totally different man. How? What happened in the "locker room"?

Peter was given new equipment. Before Jesus died, He clarified to the disciples that He was not abandoning them. In fact, he said it was "good" that He was leaving them because He would return in a different form. That new form is the Holy Spirit. Simply put, the Holy Spirit is not some ghost but the very Spirit of Jesus that comes to live inside your mind, heart and will. Paul said, "This is the secret: that Christ in your hearts is your only hope of glory" (Colossians 1:27 TLB).

In our own strength, we have no hope of successfully living the Christian life. Jesus told the disciples not to try to work for Him until the Holy Spirit was given because "you will receive power when the Holy Spirit comes on you" (Acts 1:8). Only the Holy Spirit can provide you with the equipment you need to live for Him.

## TWO KINDS OF CHRISTIANS

Catherine Marshall gives profound insight as she distinguishes between two kinds of Christians: those who only have the Lord Jesus with them and those who have Christ in them.

"The first group of Christians must still handle the knotty problems of their lives on their own strength, with Jesus' help. They get much help, of course, for a loving Lord will always give us all we allow Him to give. So that is good, yet not good enough.

"The second group knows that they are helpless as Jesus said. They also know that the 'vine life' is the only one that is going to bring heaven's power to earth and get results ... This inside life is what the Spirit makes possible to us."[4]

Do you know which group you're in? As a believer, perhaps you switch back and forth.

Peter switched groups. Because he failed so profoundly, he understood his need for the kind of power only God can provide.

"We live in a world that is seeking power—power to cope, power to propel us beyond the level of mere existence, power to overcome life's problems, power to live life at peak ... Jesus bequeaths us such power, magnificent power, power to raise the dead, to heal the sick, to overcome and to endure. That power is the Holy Spirit. Over three hundred times in the New Testament the Holy Spirit is associated with power. You and I, therefore, have not scratched the surface with regard to what is available to us through the Holy Spirit."[5]

## FROM SAND TO ROCK

When the power of the Holy Spirit entered in Peter's life, it exploded and dramatically changed the second half.

The next time we see him, he is addressing a large crowd of people gathered in Jerusalem. His mouth, which had always gotten him into trouble, has now been transformed by the Holy Spirit. His message is electrifying, fearless, and commanding. When the religious leaders "saw the boldness of Peter and John, and could see that they were obviously uneducated non-professionals, they were amazed and realized what being with Jesus had done for them!" (Acts 4:13 TLB).

The result of Peter's preaching? Three thousand people had been "cut to the heart" and saved. (See Acts 2:40–41.) This fulfilled the prophecy that Peter would become a "fisher of men" because this time the nets brimmed over with the souls of men.

Consider the differences we see in Peter after he received the Holy Spirit:

**Learning to Pray.** Following this event, we observe that Peter had developed a consistent, disciplined time for prayer each day (Acts 3:1). How amazing, coming from a man known for being inconsistent, undisciplined and so weak he could not stay awake to pray with Jesus the night before He died.

**An Instrument of Healing.** When confronted by a lame beggar, he offered to heal the man. While the former Peter would have been highly pleased with himself, Scripture reveals that he took no credit at all for himself—not even a 10% cut! He gave the praise to God alone. The boastful, prideful spirit of Peter had been transformed (Acts 3:2–10).

**Standing Strong under Pressure.** A second time a crowd gathered and Peter seized another opportunity to preach, 2,000 more believers were added to the church. Because of this, he was arrested, put in jail, and commanded to stop preaching. Previously he would have folded under this kind of pressure. Now, no threats or pressure from the religious leaders caused Peter to waver, shift or get angry. His mind was calm, his emotions under control. Such strength and wisdom is totally new for the fisherman. (See Acts 3:11—4:4.)

**Unwavering Loyalty.** Days later, when Peter and other apostles were arrested and commanded to stop preaching about Jesus, Peter and the others replied, "We must obey God rather than men!" (Acts 5:29). Even though the religious leaders threatened to kill him, Peter was no longer "shifting sand." And in spite of being severely beaten, he and the others "left the Council chamber rejoicing that God had counted them worthy to suffer dishonor for his name" (Acts 5:41 TLB).

Where is the angry spirit that cursed and slashed off the ear of the temple guard? Where is the coward who wanted to avoid suffering at all costs? Even today he speaks to us through the letter he wrote: "If you suffer as a Christian … praise God that you bear that name" (1 *Peter* 4:16). When Jesus' Spirit indwells you, He will produce, in increasing measure, the fruit of love, joy, peace, patience, kindness, goodness, faithfulness, gentleness and self-control. (See Galatians 5:22–23.)

**Leader in the New Church.** The one who had shifted out of cowardice, disloyalty and failure, is now the rock—the pillar of strength for the early church. When there were heated arguments, it was Peter and the other leaders who settled them with gentleness, wisdom, and maturity. (See Acts 15:1–11.) Instead of bursting out with impatient, impulsive behavior, Peter demonstrated leadership with loving authority and skill.

When God needed Peter to take the gospel to all people—not just the Jews—Peter did not base his decision on personal preferences. By following the Holy Spirit, he was able to set aside years of deep prejudice and antagonism against Gentiles. Not only was Peter's "mouth" changed, but his arrogance and pride were transformed into humility. Anger and revenge disappeared into peace and love. Cowardice and fear were transformed into faith. Through this crude, illiterate man, the Holy Spirit has given us two books of the Bible that reveal profound truths about trouble, suffering, humility, and holiness.

## REACHING THE TOP AT THE BOTTOM

While each threat to his life became more severe, Peter never stopped spreading Christianity. He never "shifted" in order to protect himself or save his life. Thus, as an older man now, Peter's life did end with an arrest by the Roman government for continuing to lead the church. His death in AD 64 reveals just how dramatically he was transformed: "He pleaded to be crucified upside-down because he wasn't worthy to die as His Lord had died."[6] He became like Jesus.

Peter understood that "down" was the direction of greatness, because the bottom of the pyramid was the closest place he could possibly be to Jesus, the Son of God.

The Son of God became man so that people like Peter and you me can become sons of God.

## HIS PART ...

... is to change us. Peter is our glimpse of just how much God can change the life yielded to Him. Only the supernatural power of the Holy Spirit can make you like Jesus. Do not try this on your own! You will burn out and give up. Only God can deposit the gift of His divine nature into your life.

You may never break a four-minute mile, but what the Lord did for Peter is not beyond your reach. How is this possible? Peter tells us himself in his own words: "His divine power has given us *everything* we need for life and godliness ... His very great and precious promises so you ... may participate in the divine nature" (2 *Peter* 1: –4). Now your aim is Peter's aim, and each day His image in you can become sharper and clearer. No need to think of yourself as better than someone else—just a better person than who you were the day before.

## YOUR PART ...

... is to place yourself in His hands. Sound scary? It does until you do it. After that nothing else makes any sense at all. The Lord does not wish to change the *personality* He gave you but to transform your *character* into His likeness.

If Peter had not met the Lord and followed Him, he would have stayed a fisherman and that's all he would have been—just a fisherman, unknown to anyone today. Instead, the life of this one simple man has now impacted people all over the world for more than 2,000 years.

Here lies the real challenge. I have seen people walk the fence their entire lives, wanting part of God but more of the world. They settle for a mediocre walk with God instead of an extraordinary walk. They are content to give the Lord the margins of their lives but never the core. They never depart from the sins that limit their lives.

**Get Real:**

**Will you be content to walk the fence your entire life, wanting part of God but more of the world?**

But I have also seen others who, like Peter, have allowed the Lord to make them more like Him each day.

Our part is to remain in His hands.

The story is told of a little boy who, one day observed a man sculpting a horse out of an ugly, jagged chunk of marble. Looking at the huge mass of rock the child asked, "How are you ever going to get a horse out of that?" The sculptor replied, "I simply chip away everything that doesn't look like a horse."

When you look at your life, you, too, likely wonder: "How are You ever going get me to look like Jesus?"

When my uneven life is placed in His loving hands, He will begin the creation of a new creature in Christ, sculpting, chipping, chiseling you into the unique person He created you to be. Wow...

Do you know that there are "no documented instances of anyone ever being named 'rock' in Aramaic or Greek prior to Simon"?[7] Is that exciting or what? Because Jesus saw the real Peter, He gave him a new name, custom-created to describe who he really was. And He has one for you.

And do you know that on the very spot in the old city of Jerusalem where a statue marks Peter's denial, there now stands a Christian church? Do not fear to give Him your life. God says to us, "Can't I do to you as this potter has done to his clay? As the clay is in the potter's hand, so are you in my hand" (Jeremiah 18:6 TLB).

"Paint surrenders itself to an artist and mere color becomes a beautiful picture. Marble surrenders itself to the sculptor and a mere block of expressionless marble becomes almost a living figure. Ink surrenders itself to the writer and mere fluid begins to throb with intelligence and passion ... You are never so much your own than when you are most His."[8]

Peter wrote, "As you know him better, he will give you, through his great power, everything you need for living." God has promised "to give us his own character." (See 2 Peter 1:3–4 TLB.)

He certainly did a great job with one smelly fisherman.

"They cast their nets in Galilee, just off the hills of brown;
Such happy, simple fisherfolk, before the Lord came down,
Before the Lord came down.

Contented, peaceful fisherman, before they ever knew
The peace of God that filled their hearts brimful, and
Broke them too,
Brimful, and broke them too.

Young John who trimmed the flapping sail,
Homeless in Patmos died.
Peter who hauled the teeming net,
Head down was crucified,
Head down was crucified.

The peace of God, it is no peace,
But strife closed in the sod.
Yet let us pray for but one thing;
The marv'lous peace of God,
The marv'lous peace of God."[9]

---

[1] James Russell Lowell, Quotes@www.brainyquotes.com.

[2] Bill Hybels and Rob Wilkins, *Descending Into Greatness*, Zondervan, 1993, 67.

[3] Elisabeth Elliot, "Gateway to Joy" radio broadcast.

[4] Catherine Marshall, *The Helper,* Chosen Books, 1978, 39.

[5] Robert Tuttle, Jr., *The Partakers*, Abingdon Press, 1974, 11–12.

[6] John MacArthur, *Twelve Ordinary Men,* W Publishing Group, a division of Thomas Nelson, 2002, 60.

[7] *The New Interpreter's Bible,* Volume VIII, Abingdon Press, 1995, 345.

[8] E. Stanley Jones, *Victory Through Surrender*, Abingdon Press, 1971, 33.

[9] "They Cast Their Nets," Lutheran Book of Worship, 449.

# CHAPTER 6

# BELIEVING GOD MORE THAN ANYTHING ELSE

## "A Heart that Trusts God"

*You can never please God without faith,*
*without depending on him.*
**HEBREWS 11: 6** TLB

*He knows everyone who trusts in him.*
**NAHUM 1:7** TLB

O ur son loves to surf. He will surf at 6 a.m. in the cold or rain because it's challenging and thrilling. He would consider it beyond ludicrous to stop surfing in the ocean to play in an inflatable, plastic pool. Yet every day you may be doing exactly this. It is possible that your life may be confined to the likeness of an inflatable plastic pool instead of experiencing the awesome power and wonders of the ocean.[1]

Have you ever considered the staggering truth that you can limit God? This occurs when you do not depend on Him.

## HOW WE LIMIT GOD

Psalm 78:41 says, "They ... limited the Holy One of Israel" (TLB). This verse refers to the story of the Hebrews who were slaves under the brutality of an Egyptian pharaoh. God assured them that He would intervene and deliver them from bondage. Under His protection, two million

Hebrews left Egypt for "a good and spacious land, a land flowing with milk and honey" chosen for and uniquely promised to them (Exodus 3:8).

On their journey to the Promised Land, God never failed to meet their needs for more than a year. He miraculously parted the waters of the Red Sea for His people to walk across its bed on dry ground and then closed the sea to drown the entire Egyptian army. He gave clear guidance by providing a pillar of cloud to guide them by day and a pillar of fire by night (Exodus 13:21). They always knew where to go, when to go, how far to go and where to stop. Daily, He provided manna and quail from heaven to eat and water whenever they needed it.

## SO WHAT WENT WRONG?

Yet, when they arrived at the border of the new land, instead of confidence and trust, fear and doubt began to creep in. They decided that each of the twelve family clans should send one man to scout the land and bring back a report. This was never God's idea, but He allowed Moses to send these spies (Numbers 13:1–31). Caleb, from the tribe of Judah, and Joshua, from the tribe of Ephraim, are the only spies' names we remember today.

For forty days, they investigated approximately 250 miles of territory from south to north, then re-grouped to compare their reports. They all agreed that the land was lush, overflowing and abundant. They returned with clusters of grapes so lavish that it required two men to carry them on a pole resting on their shoulders. (This image is the logo for Israel's Ministry of Tourism today.)

How luscious this must have looked to people who had traveled over a year through the desert! All twelve spies agreed that the cities were large and well-fortified, and that the current inhabitants were numerous and strong.

But then the unthinkable occurred.

Going beyond their assignment to gather information, they added their own opinions based on common sense, human reasoning and fear. I'm sure they were proud of their sound logic and realistic assessment of the facts. But their conclusions were not only wrong but disastrous.

Ten of the twelve spies flatly stated, "We can't enter this land! The people who live there are like giants! They are powerful and would devour us. Beside them we felt like mere grasshoppers!" (paraphrase of Numbers 13:28–33).

Having started out in faith, they do not believe that God can finish the job.

## WHO'S THE GRASSHOPPER?

Caleb's and Joshua's hearts must have stopped. They had also seen the cities, fortifications and the strength of the people, but their conclusion was totally different. It never occurred to them that God could not be depended on to give them the land.

Caleb and Joshua said, "Look you guys! We are the giants; they are the grasshoppers! Have you forgotten who is on our side? Have you forgotten what God has done for us? He's already promised this land to us! There is no need to fear or cower! Let's go in!" (paraphrase of Numbers 13:30; 14:1–9). They had no intention of being grasshoppers in a plastic pool. They wanted the ocean and believed God more than anything else.

The other ten were so overcome with unbelief that their attitude made "the hearts of the people melt with fear" (Joshua 14:8). Believing that the majority couldn't possibly be wrong, they began to "spread a bad report" that went through the camp of two million like wildfire (Numbers 13:32).

## THE RESULT: UNBELIEVING LIVES

Satan outsmarted them by raising the doubt that God alone couldn't possibly be sufficient to conquer the land. They placed their reliance on human judgment instead of God's promise. Therefore God abruptly invaded the camp with fierce judgment. The ten spies were struck dead with a plague (Numbers 14:37). Not one person of the unbelieving generation was allowed to enter the Promised Land except for Joshua and Caleb (Numbers 14:29–30).

Why was the penalty so harsh? Because they knew exactly what God had told them to do and refused to do it. Their unbelief was contempt of His very character. They wouldn't believe God more than the men— because "the whole course of life is upset by failure to put God where He belongs. We exalt ourselves instead of God."[2]

Now they would never taste the luscious grapes or drink God's milk and honey. They spent the next forty years aimlessly circling the wilderness with scorching sun, scorpions, snakes and scarce food and water. The Hebrews settled for living in a really small world—small like grasshoppers, plastic pools, and lives that limit God.

## WHAT DO WE BELIEVE MORE THAN GOD?

The culture around us. Recently I saw a church sign that said, "If you want to hear God you have to turn down the world." So true! For too many of us it's completely normal to rely solely upon our own judgment, abilities, ambition, money, or good looks. We are self-reliant, self-sufficient, and confident we can do a better job than God.

Bookstores are flooded with self-help books because it's more normal to depend on self than on God. Unless you were taught at an early age that God alone is worthy of your complete trust—and that it is completely normal to trust Him for all things—then the world *will have* the greater influence over what you think and believe.

It staggers me the places where people put their trust besides God. In conversations we repeatedly hear people say, "Well, I think ..." We place such confidence in all of our "I thinks,"[3] which we value so highly.

But the intelligent person must ask, "Where have all of my 'I thinks' come from?" My parents, my peers, teachers, coaches; what is acceptable in the eyes of society; what makes the most sense; or what is cheaper, easier, more efficient, bigger, better or politically correct? What we "think" can change overnight since new information daily replaces the old. Thus trust can only be as reliable as the object it is placed in.

## TRUTH IS ...

"None of us had anything to do with being born; no control over our sex, nationality or color; over our ancestry, nor our basic mental or physical abilities. An autonomic nervous system controls every vital function of our body. A power that no one understands keeps our heart beating, our lungs breathing, our blood circulating, our body temperature at 98.6 degrees. A surgeon can cut tissue, but he is helpless to force the body to heal ... Self-sufficient? Hardly!"[4]

Much of what we take pride in has nothing to do with our own efforts. Anything we achieve or possess can be snatched away at any moment by illness, accident or economic collapse. Yet we still remain confident that we can handle things on our own?

Thus we begin to see the staggering truth of what Jesus meant when He said, "Apart from me you can do nothing (John 15:5). He even declared that He Himself could no nothing apart from the Father! (See John 5:19.) If *Jesus* was fully dependent on God for everything, can we do any less?

God says, "Don't try to figure everything out on your own. Listen for God's voice in everything you do, everywhere you go" (Proverbs 3:5–6 MSG). No mention of computers, iPods, the news, or what the majority of people think being what we can trust.

Once we are *convinced* of the awesome reality that He is totally sufficient, an amazing security sets in! "Anyone who trusts in him will never be disappointed" (1 Peter 2:6 NCV).

## WHO DO YOU LISTEN TO?

How easily are you swayed by the opinions of others, their practical logic, and human conclusions? Do those around you view all things merely on a human level? Or do they point you to God and encourage you to trust Him fully? Take a decisive step  now to have those friends who will help you on your way to God.

Do God and His Word have an equal or greater influence on your thinking? This is the

### Get Real:

How easily are you swayed by the opinions of others, their practical logic, and human conclusions?

most essential part of belonging to Jesus. "Trust in the LORD with all your heart and lean not on your own understanding; in all your ways acknowledge him, and He will make your paths straight. Do not be wise in your own eyes" (Proverbs 3:5–7). Notice God doesn't say *not to have* any understanding. He says *not to rely* only on your own assessment of things.

## NON-BELIEVING BELIEVERS

One author identifies unbelieving believers as: "someone who ... will arrive in heaven [but] the problem is that this person has never believed with his whole being ... with his mind ... he is a believer. And yet at the same time, he feels that he is in charge of every aspect of his Christian life ... in his emotions he is unbelieving."[5]

He goes on to say that heaven will be filled with people who were forgiven but, like the Hebrews, never experienced the life that God intended for them to have here. They are interested in Jesus but do not identify with Him.

Saved souls but wasted years. Plastic pools instead of the ocean. Another person put it this way: "About ten I accepted the generous offer of God's salvation in Christ ... Yet for the next thirty years of my young life I lived very much for myself, wandering in the wilderness of divided loyalties, divided affections, divided interests, not willing to fully submit myself to His will as 'Lord of my life' ... 'King of my will.'"[6]

> **Truth is...**
>
> It seems scary to trust in an unseen, invisible God. But the good news is that it is more foolish *not* to trust God.

In the first third of your life you will likely choose a career, a spouse, a job, as well as many of your priorities and values. Will your decisions be made from a heart that believes God more than anything else? Not looking to God first can leave you with the "sooner syndrome," meaning that one day you will say, "I wish I had trusted Him sooner!"

## HOW DO I TRUST HIM?

Perhaps you can't comprehend the idea of trusting God. Sure, it seems scary to trust in an unseen, invisible God. But the good news is that it is more foolish *not* to trust God. Never presume that being unseen means that He is unknown! That is a lie from our enemy. Understand that the visible world around us is constantly changing, breaking down, perhaps disappointing us, and even betraying our trust. If you can see it, you can lose it. Even people.

Yet when we depend on God, our lives are not precarious but solid! Psalm 125:1–2 says, "Those who trust in the LORD are like Mount Zion, which cannot be shaken but endures forever. As the mountains surround Jerusalem, so the LORD surrounds his people" (Psalm 125:1–2).

While many other cities were open and exposed to dangerous attackers, Jerusalem had the natural protection of being "set in a saucer of hills. It was the safest of cities because of the protective fortress of the hills. Just so is the person of faith! Better than a city wall, better than military fortification … are (these hills) which illustrate and enforce the reality of God's secure love and care."[7]

You are nestled in the center of His saucer.

## WHAT TRUST LOOKS LIKE

In the 1860s, a man named Charles Blondin became famous for walking across Niagara Falls in Ontario, Canada. People loved to watch him as every week he crossed the falls on a tightrope. Since people tend to want more and more thrills, one Saturday he declared he would take a man across the falls in a wheelbarrow. That morning in a local pub he heard a man say, "I believe he can do it; I guarantee he can." To which Blondin responded, "I'm so glad you have faith in me because I need someone to get in the wheelbarrow." You see "faith is getting in the wheelbarrow. Faith is staking your life and your happiness on God's truth." Do you think he got in? Of course not.[8]

Trust is leaning past the control of your own balance. It means believing God more than anything else. It is being settled in your mind that He alone knows you better than you know yourself, He alone knows the future, and He totally has your back! He alone knows what is best for your life. What could be more reliable than that?

When your heart is settled in Jesus Christ, your desire is to trust Him completely even though it is hard. You don't want to trust in anything less.

"It's wonderful what happens when Christ displaces worry at the center of your life" (Philippians 4:7 MSG).

## WHAT YOU DON'T KNOW CAN REALLY HURT YOU

Without question, the number one reason people don't trust God is because they really don't know Him. Just as you wouldn't trust a person you don't know, clearly the person who doesn't know God finds it impossible to trust Him. "Let not the wise man boast of his wisdom or the strong man boast of his strength or the rich man boast of his riches, but let him who boasts boast ... that he understands and knows me, that I am the LORD" (Jeremiah 9:23–24).

This gives you a whole new ambition. Get to know Him! Because once you do, you'll never hesitate to trust Him.

The number one boast of Caleb's life was that he knew God and believed He could handle anything.

When the Berlin wall, which had separated East Germany from West Germany for nearly thirty years, came down in 1989, the East Germans were appalled to discover that they were still locked in a lifestyle where technology, medicine, education was nearly forty years behind the rest of Germany and Europe. That wall had kept their lives small, limited, and deprived.

Likewise, if Satan can keep you ignorant of God's sufficiency, faithfulness, wisdom, and love, you will never entrust your life to God, nor will you ever know what you are missing.

The enemy will keep you away from magnificent sources where you can learn truth, things like great Christian biographies, books, teachers, and ministers, as well as camps and conferences where true faith is shared boldly. How quickly our schedules fill up before God ever has a chance to fit in. What wins out when you have to choose? Attend a Christian activity or a school function? Spend time with God or stay on your iPhone?

## WHAT IS NORMAL FOR A CHRISTIAN?

A significant truth to recognize from this story is that the "many" got it wrong and it was only the "few" who got it right. Caleb and Joshua's story sets a new standard for what is normal for the Christian whose identity is found in Jesus Christ.

## IT IS NORMAL TO KNOW GOD

The reason Caleb had "a different spirit" within him was because he knew God personally, and that changed everything! Thousands of years later, Paul also attested that the driving passion of his life was: "I want to know Christ" (Philippians 3:10). Once you really know Him and understand this, you know that you do not have to twist His arm to answer your prayers. Instead you are "laying hold of His highest willingness."[9]

The most significant way I have come to know God is through a weekly prayer group of mothers that I've been in for eighteen years. Each week we meditate on one attribute of God. The Scriptures we use teach us about God and how He works.[10] As a power protein drink is to the body, so is praying to our spirit!

We've seen kids make better choices on their own as we've prayed for them. We've prayed for safety for our kids. Car wrecks with no physical harm have added caution to our kids' driving. We've prayed for college scholarships, Christian spouses, calls into ministry, and the salvation of individuals—and seen God answer in wonderful ways.

## TO DEPEND ON GOD

Was Caleb naïve or overconfident? Scripture leaves no uncertainty regarding this question. Caleb is described by God as one who "has a different spirit; he follows me passionately" (Numbers 14:24 MSG). Caleb wholly trusted in God. He did not doubt that God would provide everything they needed. His faith was stronger than any fears.

The book *My Utmost For His Highest,* printed in 1927, is still a bestseller today. In the biography of Oswald Chambers, the author, we read, "His unspoken motto in every circumstance (was) 'I *refuse* to worry.' Without anxiety, he welcomed each day and its developments under the sovereign hand of God."[11] Those four powerful words can change our lives when we place our complete trust in a God we know personally.

"Such a man will not be overthrown by evil circumstances ... He does not fear bad news, nor live in dread of what may happen. For *he is settled in his mind* that Jehovah will take care of him. That is why he is not afraid" (Psalm 112:6–8 TLB, italics mine).

A friend of mine shares that as a young missionary in Nicaragua she fell on her bed one day and wept at the many obstacles rising up before her and her husband. Her four-year-old daughter came up to her, quietly rubbed her mother's head and said, "Mommy, don't cry. Remember to cast your cares on Him" (1 Peter 5:7). The Greek word for "cast" means to "fling" or "throw."

The mother had already taught her to observe how the island fisher-men "cast their nets" on the waters to catch fish. And she had also taught her daughter that this is how we are to cast our cares on the Lord.

## IT IS NORMAL TO KNOW SOMEONE LIKE CALEB

Guess what? I have a special friend who actually gets in the wheelbarrow. He is the Young Life director for our area, and when he spoke at our church a young person asked him what was the hardest part of his job. After a pause, he simply answered, "Trusting God." This young man, strong in his faith, was admitting that it is always a challenge to trust God daily. His honesty teaches us that learning to trust God will be a lifelong process. But "hard" doesn't cause him to stop! He would find it totally laughable to depend on anyone but God. It would never occur to Scottie to doubt God's sufficiency.

Scottie, who is so loving and basically hilarious (riding in his wheelbar-row), is one of the most encouraging people I know. Daily he trusts God to help him reach lost kids in our high schools who are growing up without fathers and students who are giving themselves away to find acceptance. He has the unspeakable joy of seeing kids place the identity of their lives in the Lord.

He relies on God for meetings with high-profile businessmen regard-ing finances and school principals who oppose the ministry. He trusts God to supply volunteer leaders who will go to ball games, track practices, and anywhere kids hang out. He depends on God for golfers in the spring and banquet sponsors in the fall to help us meet the budget. Recently our committee faced a financial deficit when $17,000 had to be raised in four weeks. All of us watched as God provided to the last penny and on time.

Our son has worked for Cru (Campus Crusade for Christ). These young people raise their own support for ministry on college campuses, in urban ghettos, and countries with strong cultures of humanism and atheism. They also minister in areas that are ninety percent Muslim. This requires wholehearted trust in the Lord. Perhaps you might receive such a calling. What would be worth more?

## IT IS NORMAL TO STUMBLE

We all get discouraged about how hard and challenging it is to live the Christian life. All of us have times when we doubt and find it difficult to rely on God in the midst of a trial. This, too, is normal for the Christian! Yet when you believe God more than anything else, you trust that everything will be all right no matter what goes wrong! You know you're not alone and that God will provide the strength you need in your weakness. Through Jesus all things are possible.

Recently, I was struggling and a good friend asked, "Danielle, can you just trust God?" With one simple question, no lectures or discussions, she nailed the main issue, leaving the choice with me. Thus I ask like the father who brought his son to Jesus: "Lord, help me overcome my unbelief!" (Mark 9:24). Think how different it would have been if the Hebrews had just prayed that prayer.

God yearns for us to trust him in the dark, through the unknown when we cannot see and do not understand. He is sufficient for every situation. Just as the gift of the land required work on the part of the Hebrews, so Jesus' gift of a new life requires effort on our part to live it out. "The sad truth is not that many have tried the Christian faith and found it wanting. The sad truth is that many have found the Christian faith difficult and left it untried."[12]

## IT IS NORMAL TO BE ACQUIRING THE SPIRIT OF JESUS

Only the few recognize that the "Standard Operating Process" is for the one who trusts in Jesus to start becoming more like Him. This may overwhelm you to the point that you say—like the ten spies—"I can't do that! I'm just a human being!" Translation: "Grasshopper."

You might even think, "Do I really want to be like Jesus? People will think I'm a fanatic … I'll be taken advantage of, made fun of … I'll never have any money, status or worldly success."

You may fear, or not understand, how a person can be wholly dependent on God like Caleb or Scottie. You think you need a back-up plan. You fear taking a stand for Jesus because you don't want to risk rejection, ridicule or losing the approval of others. You're not sure you have the courage to get up and cross the school cafeteria to sit with a different group of people who might not be so popular.

So you stay in the plastic pool instead of heading for the shining ocean. The enemy has convinced you that God alone cannot possibly be sufficient for every aspect of your life.

Think of the carcasses of those who died in the wilderness, while the gleaming land of Canaan lay within full view. The Hebrews had decided it was beyond their reach, too difficult, when God had already promised a future beyond what they could even think or imagine.

## LIVES UNLIMITED

Over the last fifteen years, nearly one-third of the kids in my church have chosen to go into some form of ministry. It still continues today. Have we brainwashed them? Have we tainted their Kool-Aid like Jim Jones did in 1978? Hardly.

The reason is that while having lots of fun, they have also experienced the presence of the Lord. "Taste and see that the LORD is good" (Psalm 34:8). Having tasted of the Lord—the milk and honey—they have discovered that nothing else satisfies them. Many of the college-aged kids have changed their majors within a year because they wanted to invest themselves into the spiritual well-being of others, the world that will last forever.

They believe that God, more than anything else, is their footing in a slippery world— their rock. Two of them have said they'd be honored to die for Christ if it came to that. One is quoted as saying, "Everyone is going to die sometime. I think it would be neat for my death to count for God."

Many of those whose professions are outside of direct ministry spend much of their time volunteering in their churches and communities. They're in Bible study groups where they are getting to know God better and where they mentor young people. They give financial support to local, national and worldwide ministries.

## ENTERING INTO HIS FULLNESS

When you believe Him more than anything else, you can leave your plastic pool and receive the exceedingly good life God desires to give you. While you may look and feel as weak as a grasshopper, when God's spirit is within you, you are a giant. "Be strong! Be courageous! Do not be afraid of them! For the Lord your God will be with you. He will neither fail you nor forsake you" (Deut 31:6 TLB). Therefore . . . what I am commanding you today is not too difficult for you or beyond your reach . . . Now choose life, so that you and your children may live and that you may love the Lord your God, listen to his voice, and hold fast to him." (Deuteronomy 30:11, 19–20, italics mine). It is the wholehearted follower who will cross the border into God's fullness.

Is it worth it? When I get there, what will I have? "The Lord himself is my inheritance, my prize. He is my food and drink, my highest joy! He guards all that is mine. He sees that I am given pleasant brooks and meadows as my share! What a wonderful inheritance!" (Psalm 16:5–6 TLB). "My soul will be satisfied as with the richest of foods; . . . because you are my help, I sing in the shadow of your wings" (Psalm 63:5, 7).

"Hold fast to him. For the Lord is your life" (Deuteronomy 30:20)— and head for the ocean.

---

[1] Allen C. Levi, "Who Wants a Plastic Pool (when you can swim in the ocean)," song, 2002.

[2] A.W. Tozer, *The Pursuit of God*, Christian Publications, 1982, 98.

[3] Evelyn Christenson, *Lord, Change Me!* Victor Books, 1977, 139.

[4] Catherine Marshall, *Adventures in Prayer*, Fleming Revell, 1975, 21–22.

[5] Michael Wells, *Sidetracked in the Wilderness*, Fleming Revell, 1991, 38–39.

[6] Alan Redpath, *Victorious Christian Living*, Revell Co., 1955, 23.

[7] Eugene Peterson, *A Long Obedience in the Same Direction*, Inter-Varsity Press, 1980, 80–81.

[8] James MacDonald , *I Really Want To Change...So, Help Me God*, Moody Publishers, 2000, 175, 176

[9] Lloyd John Ogilvie, *God's Best for My Life*, Harvest House Publishers, 1981.

[10] Moms In Touch *International Leaders Manual*.

[11] David McCasland, Oswald Chambers: *Abandoned to God*, Discovery House Publishers, 1993, 225.

[12] G.K. Chesterson, Quotes.

# CHAPTER 7

# PERCEIVING THE REAL WORLD
## *"The Heart that Sees"*

*Give your heart to the heavenly things,*
*not to the passing things of earth.*
**COLOSSIANS 3:2** PHILLIPS

A quiet-spoken, yet compelling, Christian college student once shared with a group of younger students the conflicts he experienced in high school between two different worlds—the world of school and his friends with all their activities, and his newfound world lived by faith. For two years he struggled with the tension of trying to live equally in both worlds. When asked what finally caused him to permanently settle his identity in Christ, he replied, "One day, the reality of who God is became more real to me than anything else."

One of the greatest hindrances to gaining ground in our new identity with Jesus is that so often God just doesn't seem real. His rewards are not always instant or even visible, and this can bring doubt. We find ourselves striving hard to love and please God, yet when we don't feel close to Him, we doubt if He sees or hears us at all. And we simultaneously find the lure of all that is visible around us to be enticing and inviting, pulling us further away from Jesus.

In baseball, when a player mishandles the ball, allowing the opposing team to advance a runner, it is counted as an "error." In the same way, we are more likely to commit "errors" when God doesn't seem real.

This caused problems for a young man in the book of Genesis. His idea of living was to grab what he could at the moment. He wanted what he could see, touch and smell, and did not care about the invisible, spiritual world. In fact, one day he swapped his entire future for less than ten minutes of immediate physical gratification.

Named Esau, he began fighting with his twin brother before they were even born. In the womb, he sought to dominate, and succeeded in being the firstborn. After Esau pushed his way out, probably with a swift kick to his twin's chin, the second twin came into the world "grabbing his brother's heel." Thus he was named Jacob which means "grabber."

Esau became a man of great physical vigor, a skillful hunter who roved the wild, open country. He loved the physical challenge and the excitement of the kill. Frequently he brought the meat to his father who had a taste for wild game. This is one of the reasons why his father Isaac loved Esau the best. He was a "man's man." On the other hand, Jacob was favored by their mother Rebekah, for he was a quiet man who liked to stay home among the tents.

One day Esau came in from a hunt and was "famished, Exhausted, he flopped down on a chair only to discover that Jacob had a delicious pot of bean soup cooking on the stove. The enticing aroma overcame Esau and he said he had to have the soup "right now." "Quick, let me have some of that red stew! I'm famished!" (Genesis 25:30).

Jacob, a shrewd schemer, saw an opportunity to grab something for himself and he decided to take advantage of the situation. He had something that Esau wanted immediately. But Esau had something that Jacob wanted also.

So "Jacob replied, 'First sell me your birthright'"(Genesis 25:31).

The birthright was an honored inheritance that belonged to the firstborn son, guaranteeing a double portion of all the family's land and wealth, twice as much as any other son would have. It also gave Esau authority over all other family members—a coveted position indeed! Of this position it was said, "May nations serve you and peoples bow down to you. Be lord over your brothers" Genesis 27:29)

Finally, and most significantly, the person possessing the birthright was assured of being in the genealogical line of the Messiah promised to come to Israel. The birthright could be lost through some sin or disgrace in the family, it could be sold, but once it was gone, it could never be regained.

All of this in a swap for a pot of bean soup? Surely no thinking person would make that trade! Yet, you see, to Esau the birthright wasn't that real. The actual inheritance he would receive was years away. But the bean soup ... now that was real! He wanted it immediately.

"Look, I'm about to die! Of what use is a future inheritance when I can have a meal right now?" (paraphrase of Genesis 25:32).

This is a guy who loved to risk his life in the wild country every day. Was he really concerned about dying? It's doubtful. The problem was that he couldn't wait. His lust for the bean soup immediately caused him to completely forget the value of his birthright.

In recounting the scene, the Bible gives a crass verdict: "He ate and drank, and then got up and left. So Esau despised his birthright" (Genesis 25:34). In ten minutes. After his father bestowed the birthright on his brother, Esau wept with a bitter cry. As a result, he lost 50% of his land and wealth, the position of honor and authority over all other family members, the status of priestly rule, and the coveted privilege of being in the genealogical lineage of the Messiah. All this was given away for a ten-minute bowl of soup.

"And Esau held a grudge against Jacob ... He said to himself ... 'I will kill my brother Jacob'" (Genesis 27:41). For the next twenty years, Esau lived in bitterness and resentment. Living only for what he needed at the present moment cost him a high price.

## CONSEQUENCES

It is right for us to question the methods of Jacob. Though he was a shrewd schemer, he did understand the spiritual value of the birthright and he was right to desire it intensely. When the twins were in the womb, God had told the mother that the older one, Esau, would serve the younger one, Jacob. Jacob did not steal the birthright. Esau gave it away by despising it.

Clearly, Jacob should have waited on God to fulfill His plan. In fact, God sharply disciplined Jacob after this incident. In addition, throughout

Jacob's life, God allowed him to experience being the victim of other men's schemes.

The biblical record gives an account of what became of Esau and his descendants. In total disregard for both his father's instructions and God's commands, he married heathen wives. Moving southeast to desolate mountain country, he founded the nation of Edom, which became the enemy of God's people. Over hundreds of years the nations of Edom and Israel battled repeatedly, with the Edomites gaining the reputation for being cruel and heartless.

All of this was produced by a man who could have been in the genealogical line of the Messiah. Instead in Matthew 2 we read about Herod the Great, the man so jealous of Jesus that he sought to kill him. This man was a descendant of the Edomites.[1] What a lasting price to pay for a bowl of soup.

The kingdom of God was not real to Esau.

In contrast, Jacob is still highly revered today and considered to be a father of Israel whose descendants are as numerous as the sands of the sea.

## DISREGARD FOR THE SPIRITUAL WORLD

Understand that Esau was no heathen. He was not the son of heathen parents. "If anyone was ever raised with an abundance of spiritual advantages, it was Esau."[2] He was the son of Isaac and grandson of Abraham, God's chosen men. Yet in spite of this rich spiritual heritage, his heart was not settled in the Lord. He didn't have time for spiritual things. He did not treasure his spiritual inheritance.

You too can be raised in a Christian home, exposed to Christian teaching, and yet like Esau, have no daily interest or appetite for God. God tells us that He has placed everything in the Bible for a purpose: to "teach us what is true and to make us realize what is wrong in our lives; it straightens us out and helps us do what is right" (2 Timothy 3:16 TLB).

Do you find that we also frequently make the same error that Esau did? Unlike the young man in the opening story, the spiritual world did not occupy Esau's thoughts. Thus he never understood the truth that God is more real than the world around us. Because of this, he became careless with all that God had given him.

## THE ESAU MENTALITY

The Esau mentality is rampant. No one likes to wait in a line of traffic or at a stoplight, the store, or a doctor's office. Our attention spans are now conditioned by thirty-second commercials and TV shows that solve problems in less than one hour. Our technology caters to our desire for instant service by providing fast communication, fast food, microwave meals, one- hour photo labs, and "super" stores where you can do everything from getting a haircut to buying new glasses all in one quick hour. This has been described as "today's passion for the immediate and casual … Everyone is in a hurry … and (they) want short cuts."[3]

When we are indifferent to the things of God, we live only in a one-dimensional world. We don't see the spiritual implications and realities present every day. When we yearn for instant gratification, our thoughts become, "I want to feel good now … I'm not worried about tomorrow—just give me what I need today." This makes you more vulnerable to temptation. It is taking the short view without considering the consequences.

Wanting to satisfy self—right now—can jeopardize your future. It can rob you of the potential God has placed within you to fulfill. For the satisfaction of a careless moment here, a careless decision there, you can spend years dealing with harmful consequences and hurting lives. Someone who drops out of school loses an educated career path as well as financial security.

The majority of sex education today no longer teaches the value of preserving and treasuring your moral purity. God's purpose for sex is for two to become one so that both of you will "cleave" to one another. Cleave means that you will adhere to that person, become united, cling to them (in a healthy way), and be faithful to them because now you are one. However, the new norm is that you actually don't have to wait as long as you play it safe or are "really in love." How many people can you become one with and still be you?

Like the bowl of soup, this temptation can completely blind you to God's gifts and inheritance for your lives. You can be left with a great deal of brokenness and pain from shallow commitments made simply to gratify self or someone else.

You already know there are some sexually transmitted diseases that are never fully cured. You also know that unwanted pregnancies can result. Never fall for the lie that "it's your body." That embryo may be "in" your body, but it is never your body. If that were so, how could I have a brown-eyed male with a different blood type who excels in math? I would call that an "out of the body" experience! Our bodies are not our own anyway. It all belongs to Him.

Unrestrained today is addiction to pornography, which is considered by so many as a harmless hobby. It's so easy … so accessible … like the bowl of soup. But for a friend of mine it ceased to be a hobby. A policeman escorted him to the front porch of his home one morning when it was revealed that he was downloading material at work. He is now a registered pedophile for life, has served four years in jail, lost his job, his income, his right to vote, and the relationship with his daughter and grandchildren. His wife stood beside him in love and support through his rehab but did move in order to be closer to her grandchildren.

Another "bowl of soup" might be the temptation to experiment with drugs or drink alcohol, to seek thrills such as joyriding with friends in a car, or take the challenge of trying to steal something. A deeper look into this bowl will help you understand the high price of hurting another person or result in a life-changing accident or an addiction.

Some students are tempted to cheat at school for academic success, to plagiarize from the internet, to lie to teachers, or to vandalize property. The closer look into the "bowl" reveals a dead-end path with poor grades and expulsion from school. It's not just that these behaviors result in lasting consequences; they will also cause you to miss the spiritual gifts that God has for you to receive during these great years: a great friend, a job or career opportunity, your future marriage partner. The love God desires to lavish upon your life is tailor-made exactly for you, and it is abundant.

"I want it and I want it right now" is not in the character of Jesus. Jesus never indulged Himself. Therefore, this would never be the mentality God desires for you to live by.

Not all of our desires are as obvious as hunger or sexual longing. Some are so subtle that we may not see how they too can lead us from

God's path. While Esau yearned for food, we might yearn for other God-given needs such as sleep, rest, pleasure, beauty, work, and knowledge. These desires are also given to serve our identity in Jesus, not to serve us.

When carried to excess, too much food is unhealthy and too little food can mean a person is obsessed with the desire to be thin at any costs. Too much rest can make one lazy and unproductive. Pleasure and beauty are wonderful parts of our lives, but are not big enough goals to consume excessive amounts of our time and money.

The hours and money many of us invest in recreational sports alone has become a national addiction. A good friend of mine made a conscientious decision to give up golf for a period in his life. Because it consumed so much of his time, he concluded the time would be better invested in raising his young children. His son is now a minister. Another friend, though he loved to paint, made the decision to put it aside for a while to allow for more important demands on his time. Because these men placed their identity and first love in the Lord, it changed their choices and priorities.

When we're controlled by the desire for popularity, social prestige or fun, work or knowledge, we may find ourselves trapped into living in only one dimension. Without the understanding that all truth and wisdom come from God and are for God, we can become prideful, superior, competitive, and defensive. School, academics and work can fill your life with activity, material wealth, and fine possessions, but these are the by-products of life, not life itself.

Jesus said, "You're tied down to the mundane; I'm in touch with what is beyond your horizons. You live in terms of what you see and touch. I'm living on other terms. I told you that you were missing God in all this" (John 8:23 MSG).

God created us for more than Esau's mentality. Every desire is to come underneath His umbrella so the likeness of His Son can be formed in us. Nothing less will ever grant the worth and significance we long for.

Dr. Erwin Lutzer, currently the pastor of Moody Church in Chicago, has said, "We might claim that (our American heritage) is being stolen, but it may be more accurate to say that Christians are giving it away ... The day of the casual Christian is over. No longer is it possible to drift along, hoping no tough choices will have to be made."[4]

Paul said, "For I have told you before, and I say it again now with tears in my eyes, there are many who walk along the Christian road who are really enemies of the cross of Christ. Their future is eternal loss, for their god is their appetite … and all they think about is this life here on earth" (Philippians 3:18–19 TLB).

## MAKING THE SPIRITUAL WORLD A REALITY

How can an active, thriving young person, busy with all the demands on your time learn to choose the invisible world over the visible one?

Unlike Esau, as a Christian, you need to understand that there are two worlds: one is passing and one is permanent. The passing world is the physical world around us, which most people mistakenly regard as the only real world. Yet in reality, everything in it is temporary. Another way to say this is: If you can see it, you can lose it.

John Lennon of the Beatles was gunned down one night on the streets of New York outside his apartment. After he was cremated, his wife remarked that "this man was once king of the world, now he is just a paper bag."[5]

Regardless of how neat your clothes are, how beautiful you are, how awesome your car is, or how many trophies and diplomas you earn, one day it will all be dust. While you may cling tightly to the things of this world we can see, they are not permanent. Therefore, "Don't love the world's ways. Don't love the world's goods. Love of the world squeezes out love for the Father. Practically everything that goes on in the world—wanting your own way, wanting everything for yourself, wanting to appear important—has nothing to do with the Father … but whoever does what God wants is set for eternity" (1 John 2:15–16 MSG).

Jesus said that a person who is not rich in the things of God is a fool (See Luke 12:20–21.) When your heart belongs to Him, you will invest richly in the unseen world that is permanent and eternal. These passages challenge our thinking.

## HOW CAN YOU BECOME RICH IN GOD?

**Learn How to Think as Jesus Would.** I know a young man who has a profitable career with a chemical company. Yet it was very clear in his mind that what he pours his life into one year will be replaced the next year by a new and better technology. Because he understands this truth, he chooses to invest large amounts of time sharing his faith with young people as a volunteer. He said "What I invest in the life of a young person will last forever." One job puts food on his table, but his work for Christ offers the eternal bread of life to lost teens for all eternity.

Jesus said, "Do not work for food that spoils, but for food that endures to eternal life'" (John 6:27). Jesus counsels us not to invest all our time and energies into this temporary world, which will not endure, but instead invest equally in the kingdom of God, which will last forever.

**Take Time to Be Still before God.** Learn to become intentional and proactive about making time for God. It requires effort! You will never have any more time in your life than you have today. As you get older, the responsibilities and demands of your daily life will only increase. Now is the time to establish time with God as an unaltering priority.

Despite the crowds that thronged Jesus all the time, He never gave up His time alone with the Father. We see Him praying in the early hours of the morning, throughout entire nights and late at night. If the Son of God could not live this human experience here on earth without unbroken fellowship with His Father, we are surely deceived to think we can.

Jesus instructed us to "Consider the lilies of the field and learn thoroughly" (Matthew 6:28 AMP) from them. He wants us to make note of the fact that they grow without toil or anxiety since they are fully assured that their heavenly Father will care for them. He goes on to say that it is the pagans, those who do not know God, who worry about what they will eat and drink and wear.

Clearly, Jesus wants us to see that there are two worlds. When we seek His kingdom first, then all the other things we need in this physical world will also be supplied in our lives.

But we don't have time to "consider the lilies" when every moment of our day is scheduled, planned, noisy, and crammed full of activities. We must choose to "be still" before God and alone in His presence (Psalm 46:10). God does not bow to the hectic pace of our lives. If we want to know Him, we must give Him our time.

Thus, discipline is required. Time alone with God is not optional but essential. Sure, it will be a struggle, but be assured, we will struggle more without Him! If we are truly adhered to Him, nothing will satisfy our hearts more than our alone time with our heavenly Father. As one hymn puts it: "Here, O my Lord, I see Thee face to face; here would I touch and handle things *unseen*"[6]—unseen but never unknown.

He is your shepherd. That means He has a relationship with you like the shepherd has with his sheep. He cares for you, provides for you, anoints your hurts with oil, He leads your life beside still waters and He restores your soul. He protects you from harm and retrieves you with his staff when you stray. He goes before you to show you the way, and He knows and speaks to you by name. Can your computer do this? Can a TV show or a text message do this? Spending hours on the phone? Will you turn these things off and just choose to be alone with God? It's a choice between the two worlds.

**Plan Times to Get Away with God's People.** It is essential to periodically get away from all the demands of life to spend time in authentic fellowship and worship with other Christians. Summer is a great time to take advantage of special camps, mission trips, and conferences that are available. Many churches have spring and fall retreats and participate in unique evangelistic events sponsored by varying ministries. In our area we have one that draws more than 10,000 students every January.

One evening I was in a discussion with a group of senior high kids. I asked each one to share a special time when they *knew without a doubt* that God had spoken to them, knew they had heard His voice within their spirit. Without exception, each one said their experience had occurred at a Christian camp or in some sort of retreat setting. If they had not taken the time and made it their priority to get away, they would have missed the blessing and intimacy of hearing God's voice.

I know the specific moment when God spoke to me about the reality of the spiritual world. I had attended a Christian conference with more than 2,000 people from all over the United States, and it had been an amazing four days. On the flight home, as I took my seat, a mother behind me began to curse at her son. Startled, I remember thinking, "Well, here I go—back into the 'real world.'" I sighed at the thought, when suddenly, just as clearly as if an audible voice was speaking, the Lord said, "Danielle, where you have been *is* the 'real world.' The world where I am uplifted and worshipped, where people love Me and seek My face, where they take delight in Me and obey Me, that is the real world that will last forever."

What a life-changing experience that was for me! And as wonderful as it was to seek God with my whole heart at the conference, it was even more wonderful to experience His living presence with me on that plane ride home. His Spirit personally came down and revealed within me the powerful reality of the spiritual world. Wow! And that's where Jesus said to set our minds and hearts! It changed my entire way of seeing the world around me.

"So if you're serious about living this new resurrection life with Christ, act like it. Pursue the things over which Christ presides. Don't shuffle along, eyes to the ground, absorbed with the things right in front of you. Look up, and be alert to what is going on around Christ—that's where the action is" (Colossian 3:1–2 MSG).

**Cultivate Thoughts of Praise and Gratitude.** These two attributes can totally transform your life! Much of what you think of in your life as being "luck," "coincidence," or "intuition" is in reality the hand of God working on your behalf.

I once heard someone share a story about a young girl who was kidnapped and held hostage by a man who invited five men over to rape her. One by one, as the five men were called, each man declined the offer. Everyone listening to the story commented on how "lucky" the girl was.

> **Truth is...**
>
> **Too many Christians are richer in the latest reality show on television than the Word of God.**

Yet it was clearly evident to me that it was not luck, but God's divine hand that protected that lovely girl! I couldn't believe that not one person listening mentioned that God might have been involved. When you recognize that it was God alone who protected her, an entire new dimension to life opens to you—the spiritual world.

When you begin to recognize that God indeed is in control, not only of the world, but also of your personal life, this will make your heart sing like never before. Then gratefulness and thanks to Him will come as naturally as breathing. Pure gratitude will overflow like a waterfall.

Every day thank God that you are blessed to live in a country where you have abundant clean water, toilet paper, electricity, and food. Many people are growing up without these basic necessities. You have health, medical care, and a quality of life that the majority of people in our world can't even imagine.

Millions in third-world countries do not have computers, TV, phones, or indoor plumbing. Kids, no older than ten, are often left to feed and take care of all their younger siblings while their parents work. How different would our lives be if we thanked God every time we used hot water, soap, shoes, and cars?

What might happen if we genuinely asked the Lord to show us what He wants us *to do* with all the blessings we have received? One Christmas, a young person gave the gift of a water elephant to a family in Asia. She did this in her family's name instead of giving each of them a material gift. She chose to invest in the permanent world instead of the passing one.

**Be Rich in God's Word.** Have you ever stopped to consider the people who have given their lives so that you and I can have God's Word in our hands today? Do you forget that it is a gift and privilege to be able to read God's Word freely and to worship? The spiritual world will only become real to the person who treasures His Word as life itself. It is our oxygen, our blood, our water, our food. If we don't treasure it, we are the same as Esau. We are discarding the very words of God in the same way that Esau carelessly despised his birthright.

Paul instructed: "Let the word of Christ dwell in you richly" (Colossians 3:16). Are you rich in His Word? I think of men who are captured as POWs and placed in solitary or the young female missionaries who were captured and placed in a metal container for weeks. If this happened to you, how many Scriptures would be engraved on your heart and memory to give you comfort and hope? Too many Christians are richer in the latest reality show on television than the Word of God.

"Multitudes of men spend more time shaving than on their souls;

and multitudes of women give more minutes to their makeup than to the life of the eternal spirit."[7] This is the one-dimensional, Esau mentality.

If we have time to read a magazine or the sports page, surf the internet, run, or lift weights, then we have time to read what God says. We have more leisure time today than any age in history. We have plenty of time for exercise, athletic events, movies, our computers and phones, weekend trips, and vacations. Fact is: We have time to do anything we truly want to do.

Since God instructs me to meditate on His Word day and night, this means more than merely reading a verse at night when I'm falling asleep. Each day I am to discern how His Word and truth applies to my life.

I need to ask myself these questions as I read His Word: "What is He saying here? What is He asking me to do? Is there an attitude I need to ask God to correct? A habit I need to put aside? An example to follow? A warning about something to avoid? Why have I read this today? What would it mean for me to obey this?" His truth is the compass that enables me to keep my bearings.

As a child I went to the beach every summer with my cousins. In the afternoon when we went swimming, our parents always said, "Remember that we are at the red and white striped umbrella!" That was because, in all of our fun, we had no awareness that we were steadily being pulled downstream by the undercurrents. Suddenly we'd look up and the red and white umbrella was *barely discernible*. This is happening to God's Word today. As Christians, our first priority must be to keep ourselves moored to the lifeline of His truth. Otherwise, we will drift away from it and never even know it. The result is that His Word is barely discernible as a hallmark in our lives.

**Talk to God.** Do you yearn for His perspective? Many people spend more time talking to their pets than to God. If our pursuit of a college, career or vocation leaves out prayer for God's guidance and His viewpoint, we could be laying aside our birthright as easily as Esau did. If you choose to marry someone who has little or no interest in spiritual things, you could forfeit your inheritance. These choices begin early when we're deciding who to date and how much of your time will be spent with other people who truly hunger to know God. To be careless regarding our relationship with Jesus Christ is to risk missing the reality of God's kingdom.

A good friend of mine had to miss her volleyball tournament because of a shoulder injury. Though she was very upset, it freed up her weekend so that she was able to attend a special youth retreat. Because of her one choice to spend some time alone with God, her life was completely changed. She discovered that a relationship with Jesus Christ was what her life needed most. God's love drew her to Himself. He alone knew how much she would need Him to get through her turbulent college years.

Perhaps you have someone in your life that you are concerned about but feel you don't know how to pray the right words. Here is a way to pray without words. Visualize yourself bringing that person to Jesus, like the four people who lowered their friend through a roof on a mat until he was before the Lord (Mark 2:4). No words are needed. Just visualize your friend in the presence of His loving power.

**Learn the Life Stories of Other Christians.** A story, a life, is worth a thousand words. Most of the time, God uses one life to change another life. You can't imagine the infusion of strength, comfort and courage you'll receive by reading the true-life stories of the many men and women who have actually done all of the things described in this book!

Standing in stark contrast to the Esau mentality, is a young man who did invest his life in Jesus Christ. His name was Jim Elliot and, like Esau, he was also a young man of intense passions, a robust, athletic type who was a wrestling champion in college. His major was Greek and he enjoyed debating. He also loved the out-of-doors and adventure, and did not fear danger. But unlike Esau, the passion of this man's heart was set on God.

In 1952, God's claim on his life led him to the jungles of South America where he sought to share the Gospel with the savage Auca Indians, Stone Age killers often referred to as the "worst people on earth." It was a dangerous mission with slim chances for success. No one who had previously gone in to help these tribal people had ever come out alive. Some who knew Jim did not understand how a man of such promise and potential, with so many opportunities for success, could go off to live and work in a remote jungle. The other men who went with him were also gifted scholars, orators, debaters and leaders.

After four years of tremendous work, prayer and preparation, Jim and the other four young men finally met with the Aucas for the first time on a sandy strip of beach. The missionaries were elated that through this initial encounter, the groundwork could be laid to establish a relationship through which they could begin to share their faith.

But 48 hours later, all five men lay on that sandy beach, speared to death by the Aucas. Jim was only 28.

You are likely thinking, "I would never do that! Didn't he know better? What a fool!" The best answer to those thoughts is found in Jim's own words, recorded in his journal, several years earlier: "He is no fool who gives what he cannot keep, to gain what he cannot lose."[8]

This is the antithesis of the Esau mentality. Because Esau, in seeking to grab only what he could for the moment, lost it all.

In contrast, Jim gained his full spiritual inheritance. Doing the will of God was what mattered the most to him. It was worth more to him than comfort, convenience, worldly success, and even long life itself.

**Observe the Results of Forgiveness and Love.** Forgiveness does not come easily or naturally. Our human nature always wants to strike back and to hurt the person who hurts me. If you have been treated unfairly or misunderstood by another person, then you know how difficult it is to forgive. In fact, we cannot do it in our own strength or ability. "Only the spirit of Jesus in can produce within me the ability to give up my right to hurt you for hurting me. He alone can do what I cannot do."[9] Ask Him to do it and allow Him the permission to change your heart when you cannot.

There in the sands of South America, the young woman who had been Jim's wife for only eighteen months went to the murderers of her husband to share the gospel with them. Along with other missionaries, Elisabeth and her one-year-old daughter Valerie actually moved into the jungle with the tribe. Elisabeth knew this was what Jim would have wanted, and more importantly, she knew God was telling her to do this.

## Get Real:

Where am I investing myself, my time, my energies and abilities? Which world—the passing or the permanent?

They began to learn the language of the Aucas in order to share their faith. Preserved film footage shows her cutting the hair of the man who murdered her husband. Here we see the return of good for evil. Here we see the ability of God to change a human life.

As a result, more than fifty-five years later, people are still finding God through the story of Jim's life and sacrifice. Ninety-five percent of the Auca tribe has now found salvation in Jesus Christ, including the murderers themselves. Two enemy tribes, who had made killing a way of life, now live in peace and worship regularly in the village. One of the head chiefs has become an "adopted" grandfather to Steve Saint, the son of Nate Saint who also died that day. "Grandfather" has made several trips to the United States for special events in the Saint family. About 900 Aucas are now seeking to reach the remaining Indians who have never heard the Gospel.

Jim and Elisabeth Elliot, as well as all the other missionaries, invested their lives in the kingdom of God that will never pass away. And they have gained what no one could ever take away. Eventually Elisabeth returned to the United States and God gave her nearly fifty years of ministry through speaking, teaching, radio broadcasts, and writing. Her life and her words have not only touched, but also transformed the lives of thousands upon thousands of Christians hungry for her profound and sound teaching.

These true stories inspire us to see just how real God can be in your life! Through the ministries of the Elliots, countless people have come to understand and to experience the reality of the spiritual world. Her books continue to be best sellers as each new generation discovers them. Not too long ago, I heard a young woman say that the writings of Jim and Elisabeth Elliot, which detailed their courtship, had helped her to deal with sexual temptation.

## INVESTING IN THE INVISIBLE

"Bodily fitness has a certain value, but spiritual fitness is essential both for this present life and for the life to come" (1 Timothy 4:8 PHILLIPS).

Where am I investing myself, my time, my energies and abilities? Which world—the passing or the permanent? Do I value my spiritual inheritance? Will I be one of the few to choose heaven over earth? When I devote my energies to the great, unseen values of God, I will see results that last forever!

The world we live in is very real. The suffering, the pain, the hurt, and heartache are very real indeed. So too are the beauties of our world, the delights. Who would ever want to miss out on the sweetness of watermelon, the fun of laughter, the thunder of a waterfall, or the flight of an eagle?

In the same way, there are delights in the kingdom of God that are even more awesome. Unique and beautiful, they are difficult to describe to a person who has never experienced them, but they are just as real. No one should have to miss them!

I close with a "tale of two worlds." One beautiful spring morning, I was driving to a Bible study class and my heart was so full of God's Spirit that while I was driving, I was also singing and praying (I do not recommend that you attempt this). I was so fully aware of the spiritual world that I failed to observe all the realities of our physical world! At about five miles per hour, I plowed into an oncoming vehicle. I was so distraught that I had done this to another driver and to our family car that I could not forgive myself. I kept wishing there was some way I could spare my husband from even having to pay the insurance deductible for my foolish error.

Later that night I was reading Psalm 91 before going to bed. (I highly recommend it for trying circumstances!) As I closed my Bible, an unopened envelope fell out. About three weeks before this incident, I had spoken to a women's group and one of the ladies handed me the envelope as I was leaving. I had hastily tucked it into my Bible, thinking it was simply a note of thanks. But as I opened it that night, a check also fell out. When I looked down, I was stunned to see that it was written for the exact amount of our deductible!

The next day our family took a trip for spring break. And the van was ready the day we returned. We didn't owe another dime. In God's great love and grace, His awesome faithfulness had covered my human misplay, my "error"!

The spiritual world is as real as popcorn, and it will impact and bless your daily lives as powerfully as that check in my hand.

We have the choice between God's infinitely rich plan for our lives and a bowl of soup. Each of us will choose whether we will live by the Esau mentality or the Elliot mentality.

"There's far more here than meets the eye. The things we see now are here today, gone tomorrow. But the things we can't see now will last forever" (2 Corinthians 4:18 MSG).

Now you see it, now you don't.

---

[1] Merrill F. Unger, *Unger's Bible Dictionary*, Moody Press, 1987, 470.

[2] James Montgomery Boice, Genesis: An Expositional Commentary: Vol. 2 – Genesis 12:1— 36:43, Zondervan, 1982, 265.

[3] Eugene Peterson, *A Long Obedience in the Same Direction*, Inter-Varsity Press, 1980, 12–13.

[4] Erwin Lutzer, *Where Do We Go From Here?* Moody Press, 1993, 37–38.

[5] Associated Press: News clip

[6] Horatius Bonar, "Here O My Lord, I See Thee" (1857), United Methodist Hymnal, 1989, The United Methodist Publishing House, 623.

[7] Boice, 268.

[8] Elisabeth Elliot, *Shadow of the Almighty*, Harper & Row Publishers, 1958, 15.

[9] Rev. Tony Marciano, Executive Director Charlotte Rescue Mission, *Crosspaths* radio broadcast. January 2012.

# CHAPTER 8

# CHOOSING HEAVEN OVER EARTH
## *"When the Heart Withholds"*

*What good would it do to get everything you
want and lose you, the real you?
What could you ever trade your soul for?*

**MARK 8:36** MSG

erhaps the goal most sought after by today's younger generation is to "have it all": to pursue a career, a family, material benefits, purpose, comfort, and leisure. In the classic Broadway musical, "Fiddler on the Roof," an engaged couple sings with exhilaration that now they have "everything." But there is an additional line in the song that says, "...Besides having everything, I have a little bit more ... I know what everything's for!"

While we understand the desire to have everything, the more significant question is, "What is everything for?"

## MEET A YOUNG MAN

The people in Jesus' day were no different from us today. They also had hopes, dreams, and passions. One day Jesus encountered a young man who had it all (Mark 10:17–23). Rich, ambitious, eager, and hardworking, he took pride in his achievements and position in life. He was a balanced individual who kept his life focused and under control. And an important part of being fully well-rounded was to have a spiritual dimension in his life.

He knew all the commandments and was confident that he had kept them. Identified as a ruler of the synagogue, he was not looking for a free ride. He intended to do everything that a good, religious person would do because religion was a priority to him. Thus, when he heard about Jesus, he was eager to meet Him. Jesus was a special prophet who could teach him new spiritual truths he had not heard before.

In earnest anticipation, he publicly ran up to Jesus and knelt in the dust, asking, "Good teacher, what must I do to gain eternal life?"

"What must I do?" indicates the value he placed on performance.

Jesus answered, "You know the commandments: 'Do not murder, do not commit adultery, do not steal, do not give false testimony, do not defraud, honor your father and mother.'"

You can almost hear the guy thinking, "Gee, I've already got that software. I've covered that. But what else is there?"

He presses Jesus further.

"Teacher … all these I have kept since I was a boy."

"Jesus looked at him and loved him. 'One thing you lack,' he said." The young man's heart must have pounded with excitement. He knew there was more. Now he was going to find out!

"Sell everything you have and give to the poor, and you will have treasure in heaven. Then come, follow me" (Luke 18:22).

Jesus didn't give him a special set of beliefs or a new program. He invited him to pick up and put on the team jersey that would identify him as one who belonged to Jesus. This invitation of Jesus sucked the breath out of him. He had never heard anything like this before, and it was not what he expected. We can imagine him muttering, "This does not compute." His academic questions of religion swiftly came to an end. This was more than he had bargained for.

Was Jesus after the money? No. Nowhere in the Bible are we taught that Jesus required His followers to give up their material belongings in order to be His disciples. No one has ever been saved by selling his goods or by giving money away.

Out of the deepest love, Jesus wanted this young man to understand how much more there is to living this life than following a set of commandments. Jesus challenged him to depart from his agenda and to advance God's kingdom rather than his own. Jesus called him to choose heaven over earth.

"You see, it wasn't the money that hindered the rich man; it was the self-sufficiency ... It's not just the rich who have difficulty. So do the educated, the strong, the good-looking, the popular, the religious."[1]

Despite all the good the young man had done, Jesus alone saw what he withheld. He had lived a marginal religious life but had never yielded the core of his heart to God. He wanted to keep religion in its place, keep it limited, and draw a line over which God did not have permission to step.

Once he understood this, "crest-fallen, he walked away. He was holding on tightly to a lot of things, and he couldn't bear to let go" (Matthew 19:22 MSG). He wanted eternal life, but never imagined it would require a full surrender of his life to follow Jesus.

In sports terms, we would say he chose to forfeit.

## TRUTHS REVEALED

This story reveals profound truths about what it really means for a person to belong to Jesus. It goes beyond the head knowledge of knowing the commandments and the effort to try to keep them. He wants us to be His, entirely His, to place our identity in His character and our lives into His keeping.

**Truth is...**

**It's always easier to *do* something for Jesus than to simply belong to Him.**

*First,* the person rich in the things of the world—rich in talents and abilities—tends to trust in those earthly strengths to give life its worth and value. Yet the status, money, and achievements of the rich young man did not provide him with a true sense of well-being. When we are satisfied with all the good things life can offer, when we feel comfortable and secure, we can easily lose sight of our need for God.

This means that the good things in life can rob you of the God things.

Jesus is saying, "Let go of all your self-sufficiency, pride, and control. I want to give you a whole new reason for your life! Come now and base your life and your identity on me."

The person who comes to God must have a compelling sense of need. There will never be true power, peace or understanding, and wisdom in your life without this yielding, this surrender. But unaware of his true need, the young man just couldn't do it.

*Secondly,* the un-surrendered person would rather follow a set of rules instead of a person.

It's always easier to *do* something for Jesus than to simply belong to Him. It is much easier to live by a system of beliefs than to talk and listen to the living God. Religions will require you to observe all sorts of rules and rituals that define your beliefs. Whether it be a cult or a pagan or false religion, tradition is often considered more sacred than truth. Yet this is a boring, joyless way to live.

True Christianity follows the person of Jesus Christ. We are "taken" by Him. Our hearts are now claimed by this first love. We ask Him to transform our minds to see as He sees and to think as He thinks. We are willing to relinquish the controls over our time, energy, decisions, and agenda fully to Him. Now our life's goal is to know Him and grow in His likeness.

*Thirdly,* the un-surrendered person limits God's rightful place in his life. We may want to do some of what God desires, maybe even most of what God requires, but we still want to retain the right to call the shots. We want to enjoy the benefits of religion—such as eternal life, acceptance or approval, fun in a youth group—but still keep God at a safe distance. In other words, we may have an interest in Jesus just like the young ruler, but we don't want to go this far. It is too radical or fanatic to actually wear the team jersey that makes it clear my first identity is to be a disciple of Jesus.

Too many Christians live this way. God is a part of their lives, but they intend to keep the controls. This restricts God's ability to work in our lives because "God being who and what He is, and we being who and what we are, the only thinkable relationship between us is full Lordship on His part and complete submission on ours."[2]

This alone resolves a multitude of problems!

*Lastly,* however, the un-surrendered person is unwilling to pay the cost. One of Satan's greatest ploys is to convince us that the cost of following Jesus is just too great. We think that placing identity in Jesus will narrow our life, but the truth is that it will bring our lives to their highest possible fulfillment. We fear that God might ask us to give up too much—things like our pleasures, conveniences, money, prejudices, attitudes or lifestyle. Thus we conclude, just like the rich young man, that we aren't willing to go that far.

But the person who fears what God might do does not understand who God is—that He is consummately good, always for us, and has only our best interests in His heart. When you have such doubts, come to Him and be honest about your skepticism. You can ask Him to replace your fears and your reluctance with trust and faith in His goodness.

What might be keeping you from becoming a fully identified, surrendered disciple? This is not an easy thing to do. When I came to this point in my life, several years after salvation, I was not strong enough to fully yield my life to Him. I just couldn't do it. All I could do out of my weakness was to ask Him to take my life because that was the truest desire of my heart.

Over time, I have learned of a great number of Christians who have experienced this same crisis of faith and had to ask God to take what they were too weak to give. These persons include great leaders who have impacted history for Christ. What hunk of history might be different for those around you if you, too, would relinquish all?

The young ruler wanted eternal life but concluded that the cost of choosing heaven over earth was too high for him.

## A TRUE LEGEND

One of the most impassioned, captivating coaches known to the sports world was the legendary Jim Valvano, best known as Jimmy V. He led his North Carolina State University team to an upset victory over the number-one-ranked team in the men's NCAA basketball championship in 1983. Intense and competitive, he experienced the pinnacle of worldly success and achievement.

But one day his world collapsed at the drop of one word into his life: Cancer. Terminal cancer. *Sports Illustrated* ran a feature article on "Vee's" struggle to deal with this crisis. In the article, he shared the inner pain of recognizing too late his misplaced priorities.

"Iowa State guard Justus Thigpen's jump shot was descending a good foot in front of the rim, a fine opportunity for Vee to say, 'Justus Thigpen!

Can you believe it? Who knows how much time I have left, and I've been sitting here poring over Justus Thigpen's stats in the Iowa State basketball brochure. What ... am I doing? The triviality of it just clobbers me. You get this sick and you say to yourself, "Sports means nothing," and that feels terrible. God, I devoted my whole life to it ... Day after day, year after year, I was an absolute maniac, a terrible husband and father ... for twenty-three years, I wasn't home ... I was going to make it up to them, all the time I'd been away.' His eyes welled. 'God ... it sounds so silly now' ... The most heart-wrenching statement is when he says, 'God, what a great human being I could've been if I'd had this awareness back then.'"[3]

That is true regret. We might imagine that, somewhere down the road, the young ruler could have said those very words to himself. There is a cost to following Jesus. But there is a greater cost if you don't. Misspent priorities can mean a misspent life.

Satan wants you to believe that choosing God's ways will be hard and that God will deprive you of having what you want. But it's a lie. God's intention in is to fulfill you by becoming the person He created you to be from the very beginning. When we choose to surrender, to let Him have His way with us, He realigns our priorities, our desires and our will. What we see as something to tightly clutch to protect our self-interests, the love of Jesus sees as a hindrance to our knowing Him.

He cannot impart His wonderful blessings and gifts if our hands remain tightly clinched around our toys. Because while we clutch plastic toys, He is waiting in the wings to give us the real thing.

## A PERSONAL CHOICE BETWEEN HEAVEN AND EARTH

I worked as a youth director in a church only eleven miles from the college I had attended. My steady boyfriend, who was a year behind me, was president of the student body. That fall, I eagerly looked forward to attending the most important dance of the year with him.

At the church, I was seeking to refocus the large youth group, and a retreat seemed to be the best way to start. A dynamic young minister, who lived only a few miles away, was willing to lead it. But he only had one weekend open. It turned out to be the same weekend as the dance.

I vividly recall the exact thoughts that went through my mind: "I can't let my boyfriend go with some other girl, and as president, he has to go ... This is our last big campus social event ... these things are important ... everyone's entitled to some fun! I'm sure I can find a weekend next spring when Bob can lead the retreat ... No one has to know that he could have come in the fall."

Yet I could not deny that God was clearly saying to me, "Do the retreat now." As one of His children, whose heart was spoken for, He was asking me to choose heaven over earth in spite of my conflicting emotions.

I can still see the clarity of those shining blue days, the radiance of the sun on the lake, the scent of pine, and the shimmer of the moon on the deep, rolling mountains. As a result of that retreat, eight young people committed their lives to Jesus Christ, two of the eight married each other, and two others chose a Christian spouse out of that high school youth group. More than thirty years later, they are all still happily married.

By the next spring Bob, the minister, had moved 2,000 miles away. He became one of the seven founding fathers of the renewal movement in the United Methodist Church and has traveled worldwide as an evangelist, seminary professor, and author. His life continues to have a profound impact on the lives of many today, including mine.

## Get Real:

The call of Jesus Christ to Himself is no different today just because things have changed, times are different, or you must adapt to the culture.

The two teens from that group who married each other are still my closest friends. We have participated in each other's weddings, have vacationed together, sent our kids to church camp together, and over the years have shared deep renewals of faith in numerous ways.

Do you think I have ever worried again about missing that dance? The impact of what God did that weekend is immense and ongoing. It is still changing lives as I write because those eight people have raised their own children, and now grandchildren, in the faith. The cost of a few hours on the dance floor does not even register when I contemplate what was gained—literally forever. No regrets.

## CONCLUSION FOR THE RICH YOUNG MAN

The Scripture simply says that after Jesus' words, "the man's face fell. He went away sad" (Mark 10:22). How profound! The ruler's decision to keep what he could not bear to part with *did not bring him happiness.*

This story is in three of the gospels and none say that Jesus tried to change his mind by persuasion, debating, or compromise. He did not run down the road after him or give him a couple of days to reconsider his decision.

The call of Jesus Christ to Himself is always a total call. It is no different today just because things have changed, times are different, or you must adapt to the culture. Each of us is still a sinner and there is only one provision for our misplaced love of self: the cross of Jesus Christ.

Jesus was clear about the fact that we cannot serve two masters (Matthew 6:24). We cannot serve God and self. The call to follow Jesus and become like Him, is a call to the full yielding of self, withholding nothing.

"Discipline the inner self by a complete self-surrender to God. Don't give up this thing, that thing. Give up the self and that carries everything else with it."[4] "I cannot go down any road on anything with anybody who has problems without running straight into the necessity of self- surrender. All else is marginal, this is central. I have only one remedy, for I find only one disease—self at the center, self, trying to be God."[5]

Scripture says that "Jesus looked at him [the rich young man] and loved him" (Mark 10:21). He grieves over anything that we withhold from Him because it will bind and confine our relationship with Him. It will cause us to miss the sweetness of fellowship with Him. Only when we yield all to Jesus do we begin to know the One who loves us more than we can imagine. As the refrain of a hymn says, "I will arise and go to Jesus; He will embrace me in His arm; in the arms of my dear Savior, O there are ten thousand charms."[6]

## ONE SURRENDERED LIFE

In sharp contrast to the rich young man is a young girl named Mary. Likely around age fifteen, she also had everything going for her. She was from a good, devout Jewish home, well respected and engaged to a fine man. One day, God radically invaded her world to make a claim on her life. He chose her to bear His Son to a needy world.

We know this was not easy for Mary because Scripture tell us that she was deeply disturbed and troubled (Luke 1:29). She was to become pregnant without ever having known a man. Who would believe her? Certainly not Joseph. He would immediately conclude that she had been with someone else and likely drop her immediately. What about her parents? They would be so disgraced! And the local rabbi? The penalty for such an indiscretion was death by stoning.

Could Mary pay a cost so high? Wouldn't it be easier to just keep God in His place and not allow Him to interfere with her plans and her agenda— like the rich young ruler did? Wouldn't it be easier to just say "no" to this voice of God and simply keep following the rules of the Jewish religion?

It has been said that the many will choose heaven over hell but only the few will choose heaven over earth. Mary was one of those few. She did not hedge her bets on the outcome, and there was no trace of commercial self-interest in her spirit.

Instead she said "yes" to God and allowed Him full access to her life, to do His bidding instead of her own.

Her final response was to lay her life before God saying, "I am the Lord's servant ... may it be to me as you have said" (Luke 1:38). At age fifteen, she knew the Lord well enough to know she could trust Him with all her cares and anxieties. That is why she was capable of saying, "Lord, have Your way with me." Six words that I have observed are alive and strong in the heart of every effective Christian.

Today, as thousands of copies of the Bible continue to be printed every day, we read over and over again about this remarkable young girl and the long-range consequences of her decision to withhold nothing from God.

And the rich young man—what was his name? No one knows.

We never hear of him again nor any of his accomplishments. Whatever empires he built or provinces he ruled are long gone, like a Monopoly game that has been packed away. What he chose to withhold was all he was left to hold. Any significance that his life could have had for eternity was lost forever.

There is, residing in all of us, a desire to hold onto self, but we don't have to make the same mistake. Like a mirror, this story compels us to take a look at what we withhold from our Father.

Understand that it is His love that highlights and targets what must go, and it is His love that says, "Everyone who has given up house or brothers or sisters or mother or father or children or property, for my sake and for the Good News, will receive now in return a hundred times ... And in the world to come that person will have eternal life" (Mark 10:29–30 NLT).

Despite our weaknesses and fears, we too can place our heart's treasure in Him and take the path Mary took. Our lives will count for eternity, as depicted in this poem translated from the French by Hubert Richard:

### The Baker Woman

The Baker Woman with her humble load
Received the grain of wheat from God;
For nine whole months the grain she stored:
"Behold, the handmaid of the Lord."
Bake us the Bread, Mary, Mary;
Bake us the Bread; we need to be fed ...
She baked the bread for thirty years,
By the fire of her love and the sound of her tears,
By the warmth of her heart so tender and bright,
And the bread was golden brown and light,
Bring us the Bread, Mary, Mary;
Bring us the Bread; we need to be fed.
After thirty years the bread was done;
It was taken to town by her only Son.
The soft, white bread to be given free
To the hungry people of Galilee.
Give us the bread, Mary, Mary;
Give us the bread; we need to be fed.
For thirty coins the Bread was sold;
And one thousand teeth, so cold, so cold,
Tore It to pieces on a Friday noon,
When the sun turned black, and red the moon.
Break us the bread, Mary, Mary;
Break us the bread; we need to be fed ...
But the Baker Woman's Only Son

Returned to His friends when three days had gone,
On the road which to Emmaus led.
And they knew Him in the breaking of bread.
Lift up your head, Mary, Mary;
Lift up your head; we all shall be fed.
**—Anonymous**

No regrets here. "Aim at heaven and you will get earth thrown in. Aim at earth and you will get neither."[7]

How about it? When you "have everything," will you know what it's for? It's all for Him.

---

[1] Peter Marshall, Keys to Revival: "The Price of Real Christianity," tape #PM-126, Peter Marshall Ministries.

[2] A.W. Tozer, *The Pursuit of God*, Christian Publications, 1982, 93–93.

[3] Gary Smith, "As Time Runs Out," *Sports Illustrated*, January 11, 1993, 10.

[4] E. Stanley Jones, *The Way*, Abingdon-Cokesbury Press, 1946, 222.

[5] E. Stanley Jones, *Victory Through Surrender*, Abingdon Press, 1961, 14.

[6] Refrain Anonymous, The Worshipping Church, A Hymnal, "Come ye Sinners Poor and Needy," Hope Publishing Company, 1990, 451.

[7] C.S. Lewis. 1-Famous-Quotes.com, Gledhill Enterprises, 2011.

# CHAPTER 9

# KEEPING AN UNDIVIDED HEART
## "The Temptation to Compromise"

*Dear children, keep away from anything
that might take God's place in your hearts.*
1 JOHN 5:21 TLB

All of us mess up. In football, nothing upsets the fans more than watching a runner who is making great strides downfield suddenly lose the ball. The guy who looked so great just seconds before is now eating dirt while one whole side of the stadium is happily gloating over his mistake.

This also occurs in our Christian walk. We can get off to a great start, and even be gaining ground down the field, when suddenly we find ourselves face down in the mud, smothered by our opponent. Worst of all, we've lost the ball.

My son experienced this kind of dismay when he learned that a good friend, active in leading Bible study groups on campus, switched to a different group of friends so he could join the partying lifestyle. Another friend, who had been in church all of her life, decided that she was tired of sexual purity and chose to become sexually active. A high school boy, who had the desire to follow Christ, was in a Bible study one day andtwo days later was passed out drunk at a high school basketball game.

"Why can't I do better?" is one of the most agonizing questions for those of us who seriously seek to be disciples of Jesus. Be comforted that you are not alone in this. The powerful evangelist Dwight L. Moody said,

"I have had more trouble with D.L. Moody than with any other man who has crossed my path."[1] Paul experienced the same dilemma and describes it in detail in Romans chapter 7.

## RUNNING WITH THE BALL

This also happened to a young man in the Bible who from birth was given divine blessing and supernatural strength from God. He was "set apart" from those around him by taking special vows not to drink wine, touch a dead body, or cut his hair. Though these rules may sound silly or superficial to us, they did represent vows he made to God. His most outstanding feature became long flowing hair.

Standing "head and shoulders above" most other young men, Samson was the first Hebrew to stand up to the Philistines, an aggressive enemy who wanted to destroy Israel. Equipped by God with special abilities to deal with this crisis, God intended for Samson to be the leader who would protect and defend His people. But the story did not go as God had planned. Something went wrong.

His story is supposed to be about strength, but instead Samson is known for his weakness. The guy most likely to succeed, destined by God to accomplish mighty deeds, lost the ball.

What would cause a person who was so consecrated, and so gifted, to fall so far?

## Truth is...

Spiritual Attention Deficit Disorder is caused by tolerating sin instead of turning from it.

## S.A.D.D.

Samson had "Spiritual Attention Deficit Disorder." He was easily distracted, easily led astray and couldn't stay focused on Jesus.

What causes S.A.D.D.?

Tolerating sin instead of turning from it.

Like Samson, our separation from sin must be clear and intentional. "God's plan is to make you holy" (1 Thessalonians 4:3 PHILLIPS). That means you and I have to learn how to recognize sin in our lives. This requires us to be watchful and diligent. Yet Samson was the opposite of diligent. He settled for sloppy living. Instead of dealing with the issues that caused spiritual flabbiness, he relaxed in his rebellion and became de-sensitized to his sin. It no longer brought conviction or repentance.

Most of us value physical fitness. We're not content with mediocrity. Coaches work daily to keep their players fit. Ineptness and careless moves are not tolerated.

Yet when it comes to our spiritual lives, we are often like the man who realized that instead of making it his aim not to sin, his real aim was "not to sin very much."[2]

"God does not require a perfect, sinless life to have fellowship with Him, but He does require we be serious about holiness, that we grieve over sin in our lives instead of justifying it, and that we earnestly pursue holiness as a way of life."[3]

The more we allow sin to remain in our lives, the more sin becomes acceptable and normal.

Sin's power over us will be equal to the degree of pleasure we take in it. We may know some people who habitually come to the altar to re-dedicate their lives to the Lord. Instead of focusing on re-dedication, it might be wiser for them to deal with the specific sins that drew them away from loving God in the first place.

**Get Real:**

What in your life takes away your relish for God?

## RECOGNIZING OUR SIN

Susanna Wesley described sin this way: "If anything weakens your reasoning, impairs the tenderness of your conscience, obscures your sense of God, or takes away your relish for spiritual things—in short, if anything increases the power and the authority of the flesh over the Spirit, that to you becomes sin, however good it is in itself."[4]

What in your life takes away your relish for God? What eclipses your affection for Him? What increases the power of the flesh over the Spirit? What smudges your identity in Jesus?

It's not always easy to recognize our sin. Pride will blind us to our true condition, and we will continually justify ourselves.

"The heart is also deceitful. It excuses, rationalizes, and justifies our actions. It blinds us to entire areas of sin in our lives. It causes us to deal with sin using only half measures, or to think that mental assent to the Word of God is the same as obedience."[5]

One of the greatest signs of spiritual maturity is the degree to which you learn to hate your sin. If a car splashes you with mud while walking down the street at night, you may look down and conclude you look okay because in the dark you cannot see the stains. However, as you come under a streetlight or into your home, you become shocked at what you see! New light reveals what the darkness covered. Likewise, only the light from God's Word will reveal the smudges and stains within us.

## TURNING THE LIGHT ON SELFISHNESS

Samson's life tells us the story of a young man who played around with what God had given him. He used for self what God had given him to benefit others.

When he was denied the bride he wanted, in a fit of rage he tied 300 foxes tail to tail and placed a blazing torch on each pair. He sent the foxes to run through the fields of the Philistines to burn up all their grain and olive orchards.

"Clever though the exploit was, it was a stunt. It was not part of a campaign against a grim and tenacious enemy … the muscular young Nazirite led a series of impromptu raids—never a well-planned campaign calculated to win permanent victory."[6]

This was hardly the way God intended for him to use his unique abilities of intelligence and strength!

## WHAT ABOUT YOU?

Just as with Samson, God wants us to use our gifts to advance His kingdom, not merely our own. Are you asking Him what He would have you to do with your gifts? He has a purpose and a plan that you will only discover through a personal relationship with Him. Each of us has been given unique abilities by God. Have you asked Him, "God, What do You want me to do with these talents?"

Jay Kesler, who has worked with young people for more than thirty years says, "I look around a room of Christian kids and wonder, 'Could there be a cure for cancer in this room? Could there be a great piece of music? Could there be a novel as great as *War and Peace*? But it won't happen if you don't give your mind to God. Where do you think Jonas Salk, who discovered the vaccine for polio, would be if he had your attitude in chemistry?"[7]

Some of you are blessed with good looks that automatically attract other people. Some have winsome personalities that make others feel very comfortable and accepted. Others are gifted with the ability to communicate or have a special sensitivity to the needs of those around them. Those who love animals could consider a ministry of training dogs for the blind or therapy dogs for handicapped children or nursing home residents. Some of you have the ability to speak another language that could be used on a mission trip.

## TURNING THE LIGHT ON WILLFUL DESIRES

While the Philistine troops were threatening the borders of Canaan, Samson was pre-occupied. Without hesitation, he demanded that a young Philistine woman be taken as a wife for him. Though his parents had clearly instructed him not to marry out of his faith, Samson arrogantly declared, "Get her for me. She's the right one for me" (Judges 14:2–3).

This cocky attitude revealed a lack of honor for his parents and their faith. It also revealed a divided heart. Samson did not recognize his demanding spirit as a sin nor his personal desire to be served rather than to serve. He had no regard for the opinions and thoughts of others.

"The tragedy of Samson's life was that he used for unworthy ends the power which God had given him. Realizing that his strength came from God he yet used it for destruction, for lust, for revenge. He acted as if God had given him the strength for his own ends rather than God's."[8]

## TURNING THE LIGHT ON SELF-INDULGENCE

Lastly, Samson indulged his desires with a girl named Delilah. This Philistine woman was so appealing that he had to have her. Conquering

Philistines was nothing compared to conquering her. His desire for her mattered to him more than anything else.

But the Philistines were out to get this guy who had torched their grain fields and vineyards. Their inability to capture him drove them mad. "Can nothing stop this man? What makes him so strong?" He continued to escape every trap they set for him.

Finally, the five heads of the Philistine nation came together and promised Delilah a great deal of money to discover the source of Samson's strength. Now Delilah was no ordinary woman. Beautiful yet calculating, a master of feminine wiles, she began to coax, plead and pout to discover the secret of his strength.

"'Please tell me, Samson, why you are so strong,' she pleaded. 'I don't think anyone could ever capture you!'" (Judges 16:6 TLB). Samson, who did not take her seriously at all, merely made a game out of it. All he cared about was keeping her happy so she would fulfill him sexually.

"'Well,' Samson replied, 'if I were tied with seven raw-leather bowstrings, I would become as weak as anyone else.'" (v. 7).

So once he was asleep, Delilah bound him with seven wet strings provided by the Philistines. She then shouted out, "Samson! The Philistines are here!" (v. 9).

With one quick pop, he easily snapped the bowstrings "like cotton thread" (v. 9).

Instead of wising up, Samson continued to play around with Delilah. Twice again he awakened from a deep sleep to discover that she had betrayed him, once by tying him with new ropes and once by weaving his hair into a loom. Both times she shouted, "Samson! The Philistines are here!" and again he mocked her by breaking the ropes like "spiderwebs" (v. 12) and breaking the loom (v. 14).

But Delilah persisted. Every day she continued to whine and accuse. "She nagged at him every day until he couldn't stand it any longer and finally told her is secret" (v. 16). He wanted to hush her up so he could enjoy her again, so he finally gave away the secret to his strength.

"'My hair has never been cut,' he confessed, 'for I've been a Nazirite to God since before my birth. If my hair were cut, my strength would leave me, and I would become as weak as anyone else'" (v. 17). And then he fell asleep in her lap (v. 19).

This time, the Philistines brought in a barber to cut off his hair. Delilah screamed, "The Philistines are here to capture you, Samson!' And he woke up and thought, 'I will do as before; I'll just shake myself free.' But he didn't realize that the Lord had left him" (v. 20). His heart had been divided too long.

The result was tragic: "So the Philistines captured him and gouged out his eyes and took him to Gaza, where he was bound with bronze chains and made to grind grain in the prison" (v. 21).

Delilah had her money and the Philistines had their prize. While Samson's hair wasn't really the source of his strength, it did represent his last remaining consecration to God. Samson had gratified himself but lost it all.

The golden boy "most likely to succeed," with every possibility for success, was now blind, impoverished, and reduced to performing the humiliating duty of a beast of burden—pushing a wooden bar in a circle all day to grind grain. To add insult, the Philistines brought him out at their parties so they could laugh and make sport of him (Judges 16:27).

## ALL I WANNA DO IS HAVE SOME FUN

Today we place a high priority on fun. And that is great! No one will be attracted to a Christian who doesn't enjoy life. Joy will be one of our most distinguishing characteristics when we belong to God! He is not out to see what He can take away from us. He is the abundant giver of every good and perfect gift.

It is Satan who wants you to believe that *God is out to deprive you* and to withhold fun. It is Satan who wants you to question if God is really good and to doubt if living for Him will really make you happy.

While everyone around us is focused on self-gratification and self-fulfillment, God's focus is on true pleasure, refreshment, and joy. These are the by-products of being in a right relationship with Him and with others. Since our goal is for His character to be formed in us, we can simply ask ourselves: "Would Jesus enjoy doing this as much as I do?"

If the answer is "no," then you are being pulled between two desires. You can go your own way without Him, as Samson did, but pursuing "fun" without God's blessing will tear you apart. It will produce regret and can cause you to miss God's best as it did for Samson.

Since God created the heavens, earth, mountains and seas, every living creature including you and me, do you believe that He can handle the issue of "fun" in your life? Are you willing to give Him a try? You will experience what one writer described years ago:

"He (Jesus) brought new friendships, new excitement, new joys, laughter and music have been ringing in the house ever since. With a twinkle in his (Jesus) eye, he smiled, 'You thought that with me around you wouldn't have much fun, didn't you? Remember, I have come that my joy may be in you, and that your joy may be full' (John 15:11)."[9]

## COMPROMISING THE CHARACTER OF CHRIST

One of the saddest commentaries on Samson's life is the verse that says, "But he did not know that the LORD had left him" (Judges 16:20). He never saw until the end how far his life had deteriorated.

We, too, can become so de-sensitized to impurity and self-gratification that we no longer recognize it as sin. Yet the truths from God's Word remain unchanging and uncompromising.

Jerry Bridges says that it is time for Christians to face up to the responsibility for holiness. "Too often we say we are 'defeated'; we are simply disobedient! ... When I say I am defeated by some sin, I am unconsciously slipping out from under my responsibility. Saying something outside of me has defeated me. But when I am disobedient, that places the responsibility for my sin squarely on me ...There is no point in praying for victory over temptation if we are not willing to make a commitment to say no to it."[10]

## FORMS OF COMPROMISE

Dating has become a recreational sport, used for entertainment instead of a holy pursuit for a lifelong mate as it is intended to be. Solomon, one of the wisest and wealthiest men who ever lived, also suffered from S.A.D.D. as he allowed heathen women to erode his love for God and even turn his heart to false idols. Is it a priority to you to heed Paul's warning not to marry a person whose heart does not also find its identity in Christ, who does not hunger and thirst for righteousness? Check out 2 Corinthians 6:14–18.

Another compromise is the sacredness of the male/female relationship that God blessed with the instruction to be fruitful and multiply. Today we not only accept men with men, women with women, but we also have parades and protests for the rights of these relationships that cannot reproduce as God intended. The Lord calls same sex lust unnatural (Romans 1:26–27). Are you allowing Him to keep making those calls?

Are you watchful about the websites, texting, movies, and music to which you expose yourself? Unless you have a strong counter-thought life, the world can quickly divide the desires of your hearts. Even so-called "family friendly" media portray attitudes that are far from honoring to parents or other people. It is currently popular to emasculate the image of men in order to make them look stupid.

When you are growing the character of Christ through obedience to Him, you will be known to be honest, pleasant and considerate of others in your personal life. If you're living at home, this includes your parents and siblings. If you live away from home with a roommate, you will to do your full share of the chores, make rent payments on time, and be known for being on time so as not to waste the time of other people. These small, daily patterns are building a character that looks more like Jesus every day.

## DEALING WITH DISTRACTIONS

Samson's dedication to God was primarily a pretense. His heart for God was casual, superficial and divided. His vows to be detached from external things did not provide inner strength. That is because spiritual strength doesn't come from *detaching ourselves* from "wrong" things but instead comes from *attaching ourselves* to the person of Jesus. Herein lies the secret.

**A. Temptation will only be as strong as our identity with Christ is weak.** To "distract" is "to cause to turn away from the original focus of attention or interest … to pull in conflicting directions." When we're pulled two ways, our choice reveals what we desire most.

For instance, if my son is on his way to play point guard for his basketball team in a tournament game, there is nothing that will distract him from going—no TV show, no phone call, no invitation to go out or party—because he wants to play ball more than anything else. His identity with the team, and their season, is greater than any distraction. The athlete who is fully invested will not be as tempted to overeat, undertrain or skip practice. He is single-minded in the pursuit of his sport.

**B. Jesus blessed the "single eye."** As one minister has said, "Once you decide to follow Jesus, the rest is details."[11]

When you are single-minded, you will grow in holiness in proportion to the degree that your heart remains spoken for. You are "taken" … claimed … and identified as belonging to Jesus. Having a single eye will greatly simplify your life.

When you find yourself under sexual pressure, you are pulled two ways. On one level, you "want" this person in a sexual way. Yet on a deeper level, what you *really want more* than momentary gratification is to honor God with your body and to have no regrets. Once your identity is settled in Him, you are able to pull yourself away and out of tempting circumstances.

**C. Jesus never indulged Himself.** Today self-indulgence roars and devours like a wildfire. It is taught, promoted, encouraged and supported by every segment of our society, even some churches. How readily we Christians also do this! Samson was easily distracted into investing his life in secondary pursuits to gratify self. How profound to meditate on the fact the Jesus never indulged Himself—not even by receiving vinegar for his pain on the cross.

With your identity settled in Jesus, you have the strength to withstand temptation. God has promised that He will always provide a way out (1 Corinthians 10:13), and He will also place within you the fruit of self-control. As He exchanges your old desires with new ones, your behavior begins to line up with your heart.

## HOW CAN A YOUNG MAN STAY PURE?: OVERCOMING S.A.D.D.

Do you find yourself asking, "How can a young man stay pure?" Well, the psalmist also did (Psalm 119:9 TLB). Though the sin nature within us has been weakened and overturned, it still dwells within, attracting us toward sin. The old nature will battle within us daily.

The psalmist prayed, "LORD ... give me an undivided heart" (Psalm 86:11). He knew he needed help for his "wanter." It is our "wanter" that we must continually yield to God, asking Him to cleanse it from unholy appetites and desires. The good news is that "God is at work within you, helping you want to obey him, and then helping you do what he wants" (Philippians 2:13 TLB).

God will bring new discipline to our lives and the distractions will become less appealing. Yielding to sin will no longer feel as comfortable as it once did!

## YOU CAN OVERCOME

It has been said, "It is doubtful we can be Christian in anything unless we are Christian in everything."[12]

In contrast to Samson stands Joseph. We find the account of his life in the book of Genesis where he was seduced by the wife of an official in Pharaoh's court. Even as she begged him to lie with her, Joseph never lost his "single eye" for God. The Scripture says that when Joseph rejected her he did it boldly and consistently, and then he fled. (See Genesis 39:1–23.)

This formula for overcoming is found in James 4:7: "Submit yourselves, then, to God. Resist the devil, and he will flee from you." Claim your identity in Him (submit to God), do not hang around the devil in compromising ways (resist the devil), and he will flee from you.

Instead of tolerating sin, Joseph *turned from* it, first in his "wanter" and then in his behavior. He distanced himself from sin and compromise.

And the outcome? After a time of hardship and trial, Joseph was given the authority to rule over all of Egypt. His wise decisions, in contrast to Samson's careless choices, produced vastly different outcomes.

## FINISHING AFTER FALLING

There is one final episode in Samson's life recorded in Judges 16:23–30. Before long his hair began to grow again.

One day, the Philistine leaders declared a great festival to celebrate his capture and to gloat as they saw him there in chains. Half drunk, the people demanded, "'Bring out Samson so we can have some fun with him!'

"So he was brought from the prison and made to stand at the center of the temple, between the two pillars supporting the roof. Samson said to the boy who was leading him by the hand, 'Place my hands against the two pillars. I want to rest against them.'

"By then the temple was completely filled with people. The five Philistine leaders were there as well as three thousand people in the balconies who were watching Samson and making fun of him."

Suffering the loss of his eyes, his freedom, his dignity, his strength, and his power, the self-sufficient and proud Samson was finally humbled. He had learned the hard way that life was not meaningful apart from God.

"Then Samson prayed to the Lord and said, 'O Lord Jehovah, remember me again—please strengthen me one more time, so that I may pay back the Philistines for the loss of at least one of my eyes.'

"Then Samson pushed against the pillars with all his might. 'Let me die with the Philistines,' he prayed. And the temple crashed down upon the Philistine leaders and all the people. So those he killed at the moment of his death were more than those he had killed during his entire lifetime" (TLB).

God's plan to defeat the Philistines was still accomplished through Samson. This climactic, final act that ended Samson's life was a great victory for the Israelites.

The needless tragedy was that Samson missed out on the satisfaction of doing it God's way. He missed out on the joy, the fun and gratification of advancing God's kingdom His way. He could have lived another twenty years as a respected, honored leader of his people—a man with a family, enjoying the blessings of serving God here on earth.

Samson finally fulfilled his true identity. Looking like a common beast at the end, but in truth, the one with no eyes at all was the only one who could see a radiant beam shining through the dusty rubble. It was the glory of God. Samson had finally done what God had called him to do.

God did not spare Samson the consequences of his unwise choices, but by His grace He allowed Samson to triumph one last time.

Thousands of years later, Samson is listed in the New Testament as one of many heroes who "through acts of faith … toppled kingdoms"

(Hebrews 11:33 MSG). Despite his fumbles and turnovers of faith, he still won the game. So can we. God's grace can turn any weakness into strength.

## MODERN EXAMPLES

Samson's story shows us that even if it's the last thing we do, we can start being obedient to God. When our son Ben was a freshman in college, he was rudely awakened one morning at 4 a.m. by the campus police. His roommate was being charged and suspended for selling drugs. After the police left, as they lay in their bunks in the quiet of the morning, Ben simply said, "You know, God can do a lot with your life if you just let Him."

When you experience discouragement and think you're not making any progress whatsoever, do not conclude, "I can't do this!" That is exactly what Satan wants you to believe. But it is a lie. Sure, our times today are different, but human nature remains unchanged. So does our God. You are just beginning the lifetime process of living your life with an undivided heart for Jesus.

#1 – a girl in our youth group stood up to 17 popular girls at a sleepover to say that she intended to remain a virgin until she married. Not one other girl made that commitment. She not only made it but has kept it.

#2 – a young man I know chose not to play recreational basketball for a season until he could play without his old habits of anger and cursing, no longer compatible with his identity in Christ.

#3 – many college students have put "Covenant Eyes" on their computers to keep them accountable and their hearts away from pornography.

#4 – our oldest son and his wife dated for three years, kissing only on the face until they were married.

#5 – a girl in our youth group, who could have "played around" with lots of guys, chose to date only guys whose hearts, like hers, were also found in Jesus. They were few. But the night her future husband proposed to her, he washed her feet as a symbol of their identity in Christ as a couple.

A water skier only experiences the thrill of skiing as long as he stays connected to the boat. Samson paid a high price for getting distracted and veering off course. Separated from God, he had no power or direction. Cling to your identity in Jesus as the skier clings to the rope. And "in the wake" of God's will, you will discover far beyond what you could possibly think or imagine.

"I don't know about you, but I'm running hard for the finish line. I'm giving it everything I've got. No sloppy living for me! I'm staying alert and in top condition. I'm not going to get caught napping, telling everyone else all about it and then missing out myself" (Paul in 1 Corinthians 9:26–27 MSG).

---

[1] D.L. Moody, *The Overcoming Life,* The Moody Bible Institute of Chicago, 1994 (originally published in 1896), 32.

[2] Jerry Bridges, *The Pursuit of Holiness*, NavPress, 1978, 96.

[3] Bridges, 40–41.

[4] Dr. Robert G. Tuttle, Jr., *John Wesley: His Life and Theology*, Francis Asbury Press of     Zondervan Publishing House, 1978, 67.

[5] Bridges, 64.

[6] William Barker, *Saints and Swingers*, Fleming Revell, 1971, 29.

[7] Jay Kesler with Tim Stafford, *I Never Promised You a Disneyland*, Word, 1976, 35–36.

[8] *The Interpreter's Bible, Vol. 2*, Abingdon Press, 1953, 790–79l.

[9] Robert Boyd Munger, *My Heart—Christ's Home*, Inter-Varsity Press, l954, 217.

[10] Bridges, 84, 96.

[11] Peter Dubbleman, Pastor First Baptist Church, Apex, NC.

[12] Quotes, A.W. Tozer, 1897–1963.

# CHAPTER 10

# CHOOSING TO COME
### *"When the Heart Rebels"*

*Therefore also now, says the Lord, turn and
keep on coming to Me with all your heart ...
[until every hindrance is removed
and the broken fellowship is restored].*
JOEL 2:12 AMP

Lloyd Ogilvie, a former chaplain of the United States Senate, tells a story about watching a soccer game in Scotland between Edinburgh and Glasgow.

"One favorite player affectionately called Geordy was the target of frenzied cheers when he did the right thing and jeers when he goofed. In one particularly bad move he missed the ball and tripped over several of his fellow players. Two Scots beside me shouted a prophetic word. I'll never forget it. It applied to me and to many Christians I know. 'Geordy, Geordy, that's not the way. You're not on the way, you're in the way!'"[1]

Ever feel like you're the biggest problem in your life? Join the crowd. This has been said by every Christian saint who has ever lived, including Paul who said, "I don't have what it takes. I can will it, but I can't *do* it. I decide to do good, but I don't *really* do it; I decide not to do bad, but then I do it anyway ... I'm at the end of my rope. Is there no one who can do anything for me?" (Romans 7:18, 24 MSG).

Once you are eternally saved, nothing can snatch you from the Father's hand. You will not "lose" your salvation. However, your *fellowship* with the Lord can be broken ... broken up like potholes in a bumpy road. Hebrews 12:1 says, "Throw off everything that hinders" the Lord living His life in and through you and showing likeness to Christ. It also says that there is "the sin that so easily entangles." There are many interpretations as to what that sin might be, and I make no claim to know. But from life experience, I know the sin that repeatedly gets in my way is the sin of pride and self-will that causes me to act independently of God.

The firstborn son of Adam and Eve did exactly this. Because his heart was rebellious, he was "*in* the way" instead of "*on* the way."

## THE WAY OF CAIN

Cain was an unhappy young man. As he labored long hours over the rocky ground he tilled, he must have stewed over how wrong it was that he had to work so hard. After all, it was his parents who messed up by losing the perfect life they had in the paradise of Eden. Cain was likely angry about God's judgment of his parents' sin. Seeing himself as a victim, one can assume that he resented his circumstances and believed he was being treated unfairly. In addition, he had a bitter attitude toward his younger brother Abel. Born into identical circumstances, Abel had a heart that was thankful and submissive toward God.

One day the two brothers each brought an offering to God. "Cain brought some of the fruits of the soil as an offering to the LORD ... Abel brought fat portions from some of the firstborn of his flock. The LORD looked with favor on Abel and his offering, but on Cain and his offering he [the Lord] did not look with favor" (Genesis 4:3–5).

This is difficult to understand. It appears that God is playing favorites, being unfair and unreasonable. Shouldn't God be grateful for any gift a person might choose to offer Him?

Cain was furious, "exceedingly angry and indignant" (v. 5 AMP).

But God was eager to resolve the problem.

"The LORD said to Cain, 'Why are you angry? Why is your face downcast? If you do what is right, will you not be accepted?" (Genesis 4:6–7). Do what is right, and full fellowship will be restored! Since God encouraged Cain to do the "right thing," it's apparent that the "right thing" had been taught to Cain by his parents. Likely they had instructed their sons to bring the sacrifice of an animal to atone for sin since that was the way God had covered their sin in Eden. And the person making the offering was to also offer to God a contrite heart as Adam and Eve did.

## GOD'S FAVORITE WORD

If God had a favorite word, I believe it would be, "Come."[2] In this story, God told Cain that all he had to do was just "come." But the pride and rebellion in Cain's heart would not let him do it.

Cain's attitude was: "What difference does it make how I come to God? It's just a religious thing my parents make me do. I can make up my own religion. Why waste a good lamb? Abel is such a fool!" Since Cain was a farmer instead of a shepherd, He might have to go to his brother for a lamb. No way was he doing that. He would not submit to God.

God warns Cain that "sin is crouching at your door; it desires to have you, but you must master it (Genesis 4:7). "Sin is not a breaking of rules. It is an aggressive force like a lion ready to leap, larger than we are and takes on a life of its own."[3] The crouching sin that will destroy his life was going his own way instead of God's way (v. 7). God loved Cain just as much as Abel. But because God is holy, we cannot *come* into His presence and clutch self-will at the same time.

## RESISTANCE TO SUBMISSION

"The questions that matter in life are relatively few, and they are all answered by the words 'Come unto Me.' Not 'Do this, or don't do that'; but 'Come unto Me.' Have you ever come to Jesus? Watch the stubbornness of your heart, you will do anything rather than the one simple, childlike thing—'Come unto Me.'"[4]

Today no one wants to submit to anything. Our culture worships personal rights and autonomy. The vast majority of people believe they have the personal freedom to do whatever they want. This way of thinking produces significant problems regarding submission to, and respect for, authority in our society.

It can so easily carry over to our Christian walk. It's possible for a person to attend church, Bible studies, clubs, retreats and special events with passionate speakers, yet never actually *come* to Jesus in a submissive, repentant spirit. Multitudes of people live like Cain, making up their own religion that does not require them to submit to God.

Consider the commandment to honor your parents. When self-will rules, you will rationalize that since your parents are so different, so messed up themselves, that the Bible couldn't possibly mean for you to honor them.

A girl can read that her "beauty should not come from outer adornment ... Instead, it should be that of your inner self, the unfading beauty of a gentle and quiet spirit" (1 Peter 3:3–4) yet still rebel against it. Focused on her looks she can ignore the fact that her inner self is bossy, touchy, complaining, ungrateful, gossipy or critical. Likewise, a guy can read this and conclude "forget about inner beauty. I want good looks!"

You know that God's counsel is to date other believers as you seek a life partner, but for many it is not as important as fun or sexual attraction. Out of stubborn self-will many young people will struggle on rather than submit a matter to Jesus Christ. A person will go for counseling, talk to friends, and do everything except just *come* to Jesus for help. Even now you may be choosing to remain in an unhealthy relationship, be trapped in a bad habit or be defeated by some secret sin.

## Get Real:

**You know that you cannot *come* to Him and also stay where you are. A move toward Jesus is a decision to stop doing things your way.**

Why do we do this? Our old fleshly nature, which can be strong and stubborn, encourages us to hold tightly to our rights rather than submit to Him. Since we cannot come to Him and also stay where we are, a struggle grows within us. A move toward Jesus is a decision to stop doing things my way.

## THE RESULT OF CAIN'S REBELLION

Thus, Cain decided to take matters into his own hands. Filled with contempt and scorn, Cain "said to his brother Abel, 'Let's go out to the field'" (Genesis 4:8). (How amazing that Abel trusted his brother enough to willingly go with him.) "And while they were in the field, Cain attacked his brother Abel and killed him. Then the LORD said to Cain, 'Where is your brother Abel?'" (Genesis 4:8–9).

Note! Our gracious God is not a policeman playing "Gotcha!" He doesn't attack or even accuse Cain. He simply asks a question. God is still displaying love and mercy because He desires to reach Cain's heart.

But Cain replies defiantly, "I don't know. Is it my job to take care of my brother?" (Genesis 4:9 NCV). Cain lied to God because he knew exactly where his brother was. In John 8:44, Jesus said the devil "was a murderer from the beginning ... there is no truth in him. When he lies, he speaks his native language, for he is a liar and the father of lies." Cain denies any knowledge about Abel. Because he refused to receive God's offer of forgiveness, he now must face God as a judge. Suddenly he becomes very concerned.

## TWO KINDS OF REGRET

But his worry comes from what the Bible characterizes as "worldly sorrow." While he was irritated and provoked, he had no "godly sorrow" (2 Corinthians 7:10). Godly sorrow leads us to genuinely confess our sins and repent so our fellowship with the Lord may be restored. This is the kind of sorrow that Peter had after he had denied Jesus. He grieved deeply over his sin with godly sorrow and went on to become a leader in the early church. Total restoration.

"So Cain went out from the LORD's presence and lived in the land of Nod [wandering], east of Eden" (Genesis 4:16). While allowed to keep his earthly life and his wife, he would never again live in the presence of the Lord. He lived the rest of his life as a fearful fugitive, a wanderer, tilling ground that would never be fruitful.

But even the guilty one is met with God's grace. He places a mark on Cain as a special sign that He Himself will protect Cain's physical life from harm (Genesis 4:15). God's heart still longed for Cain to repent and return to Him.

## WHAT ABOUT YOU?

Anyone who watches ball games knows that what draws the most heat is when the referee makes a call you don't like. In the same way, we too contest the calls that God makes in our lives. We like to make up our own rules.

Is there a place in your heart where are you are contesting God's call like spectators contest the call of a ref? Maybe your priorities, a habit, an attitude, anger, resentment, or an addiction to the computer or sports, or how you choose to dress or spend your time? Have you perhaps rationalized cheating, or stealing or lying? Do you live in patterns that are judgmental, prideful, self-indulgent, or undisciplined? Have you compromised purity?

James 1:23–25 compares the Bible to a mirror because it shows us how we look on the inside, like a spiritual CAT scan. What might we see?

## THE INDEPENDENT WILL SELF-LEGISLATES

This basically means you do what you want on your own terms. Our family refers to this as "self-legislation."

When our sons refused our requests to slow down when driving in residential areas, they were self-legislating because in their words they had "everything under control." In reality, they were simply choosing to drive "their way" instead of the right way.

Self-legislators never have to do a certain thing at a given time. They always intend to do the task "later." This, however, is still self-legislation because they retain the right to determine "how much later" it will be.

A person can live their entire Christian life this way. It looks like you're obeying God, but in reality you're finding ways to keep doing only what you want to do.

If your coach asks you to run two miles every day, you run the two miles because you like this conditioning. When he requires you to lift weights for resistance strength, you lift weights every day because you value this. But when the coach asks you to jump rope 15 minutes a day, a problem arises. You hate to jump rope. So you reason that this requirement isn't really that important and doesn't apply to you. Thus you really haven't submitted at all because your own judgment remained the determining factor as to what you would or would not do.

That is self-legislation.

## THE INDEPENDENT WILL REJECTS GOD'S OFFER OF HELP

We know that God can change us. We know that His promises and power can give us a new heart. So why not go for it?

A college professor traveling through the Holy Land talks about visiting a small, local community where he noticed a group of children playing in a courtyard. Suddenly they all began yelling "Abba! Abba! Abba!" This is the warm, affectionate Hebrew word for "daddy." Their kite was caught in a tree.

The children knew that simply calling "Abba" would bring their daddy out to help. They also understood that he was the only one who could fix their problem. So "Abba" here really meant "Come Daddy, come!"

In the same way, God longs for you to call on Him, freely and quickly, when your "kite" gets stuck in a tree. But Cain refused God's help. He wasn't about to admit that he had a tremendous sin problem that only God could remedy.

When you are out of fellowship with Him, you will not turn to your Abba, "Daddy" who longs to loosen your tangled kites! If you want to know God, you must be willing to humble yourself and be eager to receive His help. He is as close as breathing, and nearer than your hands and feet.

## THE INDEPENDENT WILL JUSTIFIES SELF

It's quite easy to rationalize our sin. We can get to the point where we are so used to the dark that it starts to look like light. Proverbs says that "all the ways of a man are pure in his own eyes" (Proverbs 16:2 NKJV). This means that our own ways of thinking will *always* seem right to us. But are they right in God's eyes?

Are you willing to submit and let God have His way in your life? Are you open to recognizing that there might be some truth worth heeding in what others around you are saying? Can you receive correction without becoming defensive or justifying your actions?

It is embarrassing for me to say that not such a long time ago I found myself doing this very thing. I rationalized that "this time" my anger was justified and under no circumstances could I see myself forgiving or asking for forgiveness. My independent will put me *in* the way instead of *on* the way. And as my son would say, it "ate my lunch"—I had no peace.. Worst of all was admitting to myself that my heart was hard. I did not want to forgive.

After a long struggle, I finally just came to Jesus and bowed before Him in submission. And it was like standing under a massive waterfall, being cleansed of long-held toxins that would never pollute me again.

You just can't imagine how joyous it is on "the other side" of stubborn pride!

## THE INDEPENDENT HEART IS ABSORBED WITH SELF

This person's motto: "It's all about me!"

Like Cain, we can harbor resentment toward our circumstances. The current mind-set today is that when something isn't right, we're entitled to blame, complain, and claim our rights. Stomp your foot so to speak. However, discontent and self-pity are toxic for the Christian.

Nowhere do we find that Jesus fretted, whined, or complained. He knew there was no situation that wouldn't *serve God's purposes* (Psalm 119:91). Because God is sovereign and in control, Jesus submitted. When things got rough, He knew he was safe in His Father's hands. He knew He would never be in a situation where He could not love and serve God. Neither will we.

Remain alert to that part of you that tries to reinterpret what God has said. We like to be viewed as broad-minded and open to all viewpoints. We like to focus on self-esteem and the right to "find" ourselves within ourselves instead of in God.

Jesus said, "Those who try to hold on to their lives will give up true life. Those who give up their lives for me will hold on to true life" (Matthew 10:39 NCV).

## THE INDEPENDENT WILL HURTS OTHERS

We can't rebel in private without consequences. God knows it all and eventually the ripple effects will spread far beyond what we can ever imagine, hurting numerous people for years.

When I was a senior in high school, I learned that a youth leader whom I greatly admired had been continually unfaithful to his wife. It devastated all who knew him and was quite painful for me. When our sons were young, the same situation occurred at a large church in our community. Not only were many kids affected then, but there are still some today who will not go in any church because of that wreckage.

## THE REMEDY FOR THE INDEPENDENT WILL

In the New Testament, Jude 11 warns us not to take "the way of Cain." As long as we are hiding real guilt in our hearts and trying to cover something up, there will be no peace. Shame can bring a self-loathing that will pollute your life. Yet know that we have a God who can handle our sin! Graciously He says, "Come now, let us reason together . . . though your sins are like scarlet, they shall be as white as snow . . . if you are willing and obedient" (Isaiah 1:18–19). Even murder . . . or whatever you would fill in the blank.

The scriptures are powerful because they are so honest. This story gives us the warning that each day, sin is "crouching at your door." Each day our natural self wants to remain in control and call all the shots. All of us need daily forgiveness by God for our controlling self-centeredness.

## STAYING IN FELLOWSHIP WITH GOD

It is actually quite easy, and requires only one thing.

Once I was leading worship at a youth retreat when I said something I immediately regretted. My conscience was stricken with godly sorrow thinking, "How could I be so stupid? I've messed up with a kid here!" Yet God's voice immediately spoke within my spirit and reminded me of the story in Exodus when the angel of death passed over any house that had applied the blood of a lamb over the doorpost.

He said, "Danielle, don't you know that when I see the blood over the doorpost of your heart, my judgment passes over you *every time*?" This means every day, every mess-up. For the Christian, blood is not a symbol of death, but a symbol of vibrant life! As the old hymn (now left out of many hymnals) says, "What can wash away my sin? Nothing but the blood of Jesus." The cross is the new and last Passover. Apply it every day.

## DUST OR DINNER?

It didn't have to end this way. If Cain had simply run *to* God instead of *from* God, the whole story would be different. If he had simply humbled himself in repentance, he could have gone home to supper that night at peace with God and Abel.

Instead, his feet are kicking dust as he stomps out into the desert sunset, a bitter, complaining drifter who will find no food, fellowship, or real peace.

God loved Cain and wanted to set his kite free. He wanted to free Cain from the bondage of self that was choking the life out of him. Cain could have had that special "Abba! Father!" relationship.

All he had to do was bow his head instead of shake his fist.

Whereas Adam and Eve received God's remedy for sin, Cain rejected God. He fostered eight generations of descendants who built a large, highly developed civilization. Yet nowhere is there any mention of God.[5] In fact, the last mention of Cain's line in the Bible describes the people as arrogant, boasting of lawlessness and murder by a man named Lamech (Genesis 4:23–24). The last mention of Lamech's life is in Genesis 5:31.

## Truth is...

**The only thing that can interfere with God's will is our will.**

In contrast, God gave Adam and Eve "another child in place of Abel" (Genesis 4: 25), a son named Seth. Through Seth came a godly line of descendants who also made great cultural advances. Yet the Bible makes it clear that these descendants sought to walk with God for these people "began to call on the name of the LORD" (Genesis 4:26).

In time, God's hand was forced into judgment and destruction by flood. Genesis 6:5–6 says, "The LORD saw how great man's wickedness on the earth had become, and that every inclination of the thoughts of his heart was only evil all the time. The LORD was grieved."

In contrast, through Seth's line came Noah who built the ark to preserve life and all who would turn to God.

Hundreds of years later, it was through the line of Seth that Jesus the Messiah came.

## DINNER

"Imagine that when I arrive home one night, the neighbor kids playing in the yard with my children have been perfect angels. They have not thrown rocks, fought, or used bad language. Yet suppose my children did all of these things. At supper time, who will be invited in to eat? The neighbor children or my children? Mine, of course! But the neighbor children acted better, why are they not invited in? Because they have the wrong last name and are not my children."[6]

Today, when we live in fellowship with God, we recreate the paradise of Eden. No matter what we have done, we never have to live out of the Lord's presence because we know that we are His children, and we know we can go home to supper.

A little boy once said that his favorite words were, "Come to supper!"

Will you be able to come? Will you be called in at sunset for peace and fellowship with the Father? Not because of what you have or have not done that day, but simply because you belong to Him? My prayer for you is for you to know these truths with complete assurance from God Himself.

Today you can know the God who is saying to you now, "Here I am! I stand at the door and knock. If anyone hears my voice and opens the door, I will come in and eat with him, and he with me" (Revelation 3:20).

The choice is yours.

Just remember, supper's waiting.

[1] Lloyd John Ogilvie, *Drumbeat of Love*, Word Books, 1976, 136.

[2] Rev. Dr. Ross E. Whetstone, Sr., Aldersgate Renewal Conference Theme, 1989.

[3] Walter Brueggeman, Genesis, *A Bible Commentary for Teaching and Preaching*, John Knox Press, 1982, 57.

[4] Oswald Chambers, *My Utmost for His Highest*, June 11, Dodd, Mead, and Company, 1935.

[5] James Montgomery Boice, *Genesis: An Expositional Commentary Volume 1*, Zondervan Publishing House, 1982, 209.

[6] Michael Wells, *Sidetracked in the Wilderness*, Fleming Revell, 1991, 108.

CHAPTER 11

# ADVANCING IN THE FACE OF PRESSURE
### *"The Fortified Heart"*

*. . . [that] he may strengthen you with power
through his Spirit in your inner being.*
**EPHESIANS 3:16**

The first time I attended a statewide basketball tournament with our son was very exciting. I remember being in a crowded elevator with the athletes, parents, and coaches from all over the state. As the conversation buzzed with anticipation, one particularly zealous young coach turned to our coach and asked, "Can you handle the press?"

As we plunged from the tenth floor to the lobby, I felt a plunge inside of me. Flashing before my eyes were all the hours of hard practice, all the exercise charts, the new warm-up suits, the flags and homemade banners on our cars, the eight-hour trip. But now, in order to win, we had to handle "the press." Simply put, this is a strategy of the opposing team to prevent our team from making any progress toward the goal.

In our lives as Christians, there is always going to be pressure to keep us from making progress toward the goal. The world around us will never help us belong to Jesus. In fact, it can cause us to doubt His love and His power and basically disregard Him altogether.

The world brings pressure to turn from His ways, to compromise truth, and to trust ourselves more than Him. There is pressure to conceal our faith, to believe we can live as an "undercover" Christian, never really speaking about Jesus. Therefore, it is important to understand some truths about pressure.

## PRESSURE SERVES A PURPOSE

Many believers have the mistaken assumption that becoming a Christian means that your way will become smooth, but nothing could be further from the truth. "In this world you will have trouble" (John 16:33) are words that Jesus stated as truth.

You know that in the physical realm pressure produces fitness. Trainers say resistance training is the fastest way to improve a body. Under pressure, people can transform their physiques to unimaginable levels.

Likewise, as we learn to respond to pressure as Jesus did, it will produce spiritual fitness in us. In fact, James says, "Consider it a sheer gift, friends, when tests and challenges come at you from all sides. You know that under pressure, your faith-life is forced into the open and shows its true colors. So don't try to get out of anything prematurely. Let it do its work so you become mature and well-developed, not deficient in any way" (James 1:2–4 MSG).

Jesus said not to worry if the world doesn't like you because it didn't like Him either. Herein lies a problem, of course, because we all want approval. He never prayed for His disciples to be taken out of the world, but instead that they would remain strong in the world. Since Jesus will never ask us to do something He doesn't also equip us to do, it's good news to hear Him guarantee that we can "take heart for I have overcome the world" (John 16:33).

**Truth is...**

Jesus said not to worry if the world doesn't like you because it didn't like Him either.

He's also praying for us to be protected from the evil one whose goal is to render our faith useless (John 17:15–17).

## WHAT DETERMINES IF YOU CONQUER OR COLLAPSE?

Jay Kesler shares a powerful and helpful story.

"In 1958, a US naval submarine called the Thresher was in the Atlantic. The seamen on the ship were unaware that some of the bulkheads had not been properly welded. When the ship got to a certain depth, the bolts gave way. The men inside were fried alive by the sea water that came in as live steam. Only small pieces of the Thresher were found floating on top of the water. The tragedy occurred, not because the outside pressure was so great, but because the corresponding inner pressure gave way. The sub crumpled like a piece of paper."[1]

The times we are living in today are considered to be the worst ever, with social and moral pressures being more than it seems we can withstand. While times are different, the pressures and temptations to human nature are not new. What I do believe is different, however, is that it's not the extent of the outer pressure that gets to us. What causes us to crumple is the lack of a sufficient, corresponding inner pressure.

## A STORY ABOUT PRESSURE

There were some guys in the Old Testament who had the inner strength to withstand the severest of tests. They are described as "young men without any physical defect, handsome, showing aptitude for every kind of learning, well informed, quick to understand" (Daniel 1:4). Of noble descent, they were the cream of the crop.

But when a foreign empire invaded their homeland and reduced it to rubble, the reigning King Nebuchadnezzar captured prisoners, choosing only the finest. Daniel and three of his friends, all probably around 16, were carried off with the first group.

Thrown into a frightening upheaval, torn from their family and friends, from prestige and pleasure, they find themselves prisoners, unable to control anything. Nebuchadnezzar's plan was to train them to serve his empire. No trace of their Hebrew identity would be left as they were put through an intensive program to make them Babylonians. The worst degradation came when they had their names changed from Hebrew to Babylonian. They became known as Belteshazzar instead of Daniel, Shadrach instead of Hananiah, Meshach instead of Mishael, and Abednego instead of Azariah.

## PRESSURE TO CONFORM AND LOOK LIKE A NON-BELIEVER

They were immediately commanded to eat the king's food. For most young men it would be an honor to be offered royal meat and fine wine.

But Nebuchadnezzar's purpose was to secure their identity with the Babylonian religion. Because royal food was first consecrated to heathen gods, anyone eating it would gain the favor of the false gods.

These four teenagers faced a difficult dilemma. While eating the food would quickly bring political prominence and ease, the cost was the worship of a false god. The pressure to conform and compromise was as intense as the ocean water on that submarine. Consider the guys talking things over late at night:

**Be Reasonable:** "Hey, this is an order of the king. Disobedience could bring severe punishment, even death. No one here even knows our God. They wouldn't understand a decision to abstain, and they will be highly offended. God will understand these circumstances."

**We'd Better Look out for Ourselves:** "Hey, looks like God has forgotten us! He allowed us to be captured and carried off. Where was He then? Why should we honor Him now?"

**Use Common Sense:** "It would be stupid to turn down the finest food in the land for mere vegetables and water! What kind of teenager would do that?"

**Don't Overreact:** "The other guys who were deported aren't struggling with this decision like we are. Maybe we shouldn't make such a big deal out of it. No one will ever have to know. We can still worship God in our hearts, and He will understand that we aren't really compromising."

Perhaps you've used similar reasoning yourself.

## GAINING INNER PRESSURE

**An Unwavering Heart:** But "Daniel purposed in his heart that he would not defile himself" (Daniel 1:8 KJV). What an amazing decision! Authentic inner pressure and strength has to come from the heart. If our heart isn't in our convictions, we will cave every time. "Above all else, guard your affections. For they influence everything else in your life" (Proverbs 4:23 TLB). Our actions generally follow our affections.

Though King Nebuchadnezzar had the power to destroy their homes, families, and even their names, all the armies of Babylon could not touch what these four young men carried within themselves. It was the inner conviction that God was the first love of their hearts. The commandment to "love the LORD your God with all your heart" (Deuteronomy 6:5) was not just religious words written on a scroll, but living words written on their hearts. They would not be tempted to yield.

It is important to note that these guys did not have the support of a youth group, a counselor to talk with, or even a Bible. Yet based on their devotion for God alone, they were able—at their age and in those circumstances—to reject compromise and to honor God above all else.

It wasn't up for debate. If advancement required compromising their faith, then they weren't interested. Their God was great enough to live for, great enough to die for, and great enough to reject an order of a king for. This is our first glimpse of what it means to be fortified with inner pressure.

Are you willing to stand up regardless of the cost? Do you stand up to foul language, disrespectful attitudes toward parents and teachers, dressing to draw sexual attention? Or do you rationalize it? Can you turn off movies, music, TV shows, or websites that degrade life as God intended it to be? Are you more prone to stay undercover, concluding that it is just too hard to be different? Does your mind say, "It doesn't really matter . . . these circumstances are different"? Daniel and his friends did not. It is a heart issue to love what God loves. When our heart's identity is found in Him, we are much less likely to

## Get Real:

Does your mind say, "It doesn't really matter—these circumstances are different"?

waver because *inside* we really don't want to waver.

**The Result:** So what happened? God's promise held true.

**The immediate result was that** "at the end of the ten days they looked healthier and better nourished than any of the young men who ate the royal food" (Daniel 1:15).

**The short-term result:** "To these four young men God gave knowledge and understanding of all kinds of literature and learning. And Daniel could understand visions and dreams of all kinds" (v. 17). Daniel immediately became highly valuable to the king. His insights and wisdom brought him continual promotions.

**The long-term result:** After the designated three years had elapsed, "the king talked with them, and he found none equal to Daniel, Hananiah, Mishael and Azariah; so they entered the king's service. In every matter of wisdom and understanding about which the king questioned them, he found them ten times better than all the magicians and enchanters in his whole kingdom" (vv. 19–20).

Eventually, "the king placed Daniel in a high position and lavished many gifts on him. He made him ruler over the entire province of Babylon and placed him in charge of all its wise men. Moreover, at Daniel's request, the king appointed Shadrach, Meshach, and Abednego administrators ... while Daniel remained at the royal court" (Daniel 2:48–49).

God's way had proven solid enough to stake their life upon. Jesus promised that when we put Him first, all that we need will be given to us (Matthew 6:33). This truth supplied a power greater than the outer pressure.

Wonder what happened to the other Hebrews who faced the same test? We have no idea what became of them. If they chose to conform, they were simply absorbed into the Babylonian culture. No book of the Bible is named for them. Whatever earthly prominence they achieved is never recorded and is as long gone as the entire Babylonian Empire.

I mean, do you know any Babylonians today? What a press!

## THE SETTLED MIND

Yet the greatest commandment requires more than just our hearts. The next pressure to conform took a decidedly deadly turn.

King Nebuchadnezzar built a 90-foot tall statue of gold to be an object of worship. Shadrach, Meschach, and Abednego were now about twenty years old. (It is unknown why Daniel is not present in this story.) At the dedication of the image, the emperor commanded everyone to bow down and worship the statue as god. Anyone who refused would be thrown into a blazing furnace.

The three young men were in plain view of everyone present, including the king. Surely their God would not want them to die or to suffer. Surely their God would not expect a drastic defiance that would cost them their jobs, careers, and very lives.

A special herald mounted the platform to issue the king's command. The trumpet blasted. All backs bowed down in a sea of obedience, in outright allegiance to a false god.

That is, all, except three.

Standing bold against the sky were Shadrach, Meschach, and Abednego—despite the pressure, despite the consequences. Immediately they were seized and thrown before an outraged king who mocked them for trusting in an unknown, unseen, powerless God. In spite of his fury, the king gave them one more chance to bow down.

A second chance. At this point, most of us would hesitate, if not falter. A second temptation to conceal their faith? Might be smart to take it.

But not these three. With no hesitation or timidity they replied, "Please understand, sir, that … we will never under any circumstance serve your gods or worship the golden statue you have erected" (Daniel 3:18 TLB).

One thing they knew for sure: Doubting or denying their God would never advance their lives. As young as they were, they brought to this crisis the inner strength of a settled mind. It wasn't an option to betray their God.

Their minds had been settled prior to the test. Even if God chose not to save them, they still would not be found bowing to a false god. Their thinking was not confused but clear.

Enraged, King Nebuchadnezzar demanded the furnace be heated seven times hotter, and Shadrach, Meschach and Abednego were bound with ropes tied by the strongest men in the army.

God appears to be absent, silent. Any hope they may have held onto seemed lost. "So these men, wearing their robes, trousers, turbans and other clothes, were bound and thrown into the blazing furnace" (Daniel 3:21). So intense was the heat that the soldiers who pitched them into the fire were immediately incinerated to ashes (v. 22).

## THINKING AS GOD THINKS

We can only be as strong as what we love and are committed to. Within the greatest commandment (per Jesus in Matthew 22:37), we are also instructed to love God with all our mind.

Are you completely *settled* in your mind that God's ways are the best? Be honest. Are you fully convinced that He "has your back," your best interest at heart? Are you persuaded that only His ways will truly satisfy you? When we have this certainty, temptation will fall away as easily as a snake shedding its old skin.

When we're not fully convinced in our mind, we will be filled with inner conflict and doubt—"like a wave of the sea, blown and tossed by the wind" (James 1:6). "A double-minded [person], unstable in all he does" (v. 8) is another way that person is characterized. We can't develop inner pressure with a divided mind. Waffling keeps one foot on the pier and one in the canoe.

This is a hard place to be. You are too Christian to really enjoy sin, but too sinful to be a real Christian. Trying to live for God, yet exposing ourselves to activities, habits, or friends that are questionable will cause our inner pressure to develop a slow leak.

"I'm convinced that this is the key to mental health. A person who … isn't trying to do two things at once, is going to be pretty stable … he's made the choice. He's chosen to live for Christ."[2]

Settling in our minds that we want to live for Christ is the big "yes" that answers all other little "yeses." We no longer have to wrestle over every little situation. When our son played competitive ball, he didn't debate over whether to stay up all night before a big game. Going to bed on time was a normal consequence of his priority to play ball.

The first of the Ten Commandments says, "You shall have no other gods before Me" and the second one says, "You shall not make for yourself a carved image … you shall not bow down to them nor serve them." What part of these two commandments would one not understand? In the light of these commands, the behavior of Shadrach, Meschach, and Abednego was perfectly *normal!*

When we give that one big "yes," when we are fully persuaded that we want to think as God thinks and see as He see, then we will have the inner pressure to reject secondary gods.

## THE SETTLED MIND CHOOSES SOONER

The settled mind chooses before the pressure comes. When the trumpet blew and everyone dropped, no time was left. Likewise, decisions in life will come at us with rapid fire and we'll quickly have to answer on the basis of what is already inside of us.

This means that you must be smart enough to decide ahead of time what you will and will not do. Don't wait till you're at a party to decide what you believe about dirty dancing, alcohol, or sexting. You don't wait till you're offered the opportunity to cheat on a test or lie to a friend to decide about your convictions.

With a settled mind, it will not be difficult to walk away from entertaining little hints to compromise. When your mind is growing through God's Holy Spirit, it actually becomes easy to reject compromise because the bait has lost its appeal. Your mind and heart are settled. That's what inner pressure is all about.

## THE PEOPLE OF GOD JAM ONE

When King Nebuchadnezzar looked into the furnace, he saw an amazing scene. Not only were the three Hebrews calmly walking around unharmed, he also saw the presence of a fourth Man walking with them. A man whose form appeared to be like a son of god!

Their "seemingly groundless" hope proved to be stronger than the ropes that bound them. When they came out, all observed that "the fire had not harmed their bodies, nor was a hair of their heads singed; their robes were not scorched, and there was no smell of fire on them" (Daniel 3:27). "God's protection extended to the last hair and thread of the three—a testimony to His absolute power and control of natural forces."[3]

It proved safer to be in the fire with the Lord than to be outside the furnace without Him!

In sharp contrast, the king's men experienced no protection. The flames designed to kill the Hebrews consumed the guards. This lets us know there was nothing wrong with the furnace ... the presence of the Hebrew God could not be denied.

Nebuchadnezzar didn't even try to deny the power of Jehovah. "Praise be to the God of Shadrach, Meshach, and Abednego ... no other God can save in this way" (Daniel3:28–29).

## A FAITHFUL WILL

As powerful as the alliance of heart and mind can be, the third part of the greatest commandment is to "love the Lord your God ... with all your strength" (Mark 12:30). One final test of loyalty occurred. While Shadrach, Meshach, and Abednego were tempted to commit a deed they knew to be wrong, Daniel was tempted to discontinue a deed he knew was right.

He has now served the government for more than fifty years with great integrity. But other ruling officials were jealous and wanted to get rid of him. Since Daniel was totally "trustworthy and neither corrupt nor negligent" (Daniel 6:4), they had to devise a scheme to arrest him.

They decreed a law that for thirty days no one could pray unless it was to the Persian King Darius. Anyone found guilty of praying to another god would be thrown into a lions' den, a natural, underground cave that was home for lions who were deprived of food. At the top was a small opening.

The only thing needed for their plot to succeed was for Daniel to remain the same! These men based their entire plot solely on the godly character of Daniel!

How easy it would be to just stop praying for thirty days! After all, couldn't he just pray silently in his head? What harm would it do to lay low and not rock the boat? Yet when Daniel heard about the decree, "he went home to his upstairs room where the windows *opened* to Jerusalem. Three times a day he got down on his knees and prayed, giving thanks to his God, just as he had done before" (Daniel 6: 10). It was never a consideration that he would stop praying to his God.

The schemers immediately reported this to King Darius who personally "determined to rescue Daniel and made every effort until sundown to save him" (Daniel 6:14). But the decree could not be recalled.

The God whom Daniel served allowed him to be thrown into a lions' den. We would assume this to be the end of Daniel's life.

Instead, it was a bad night for King Darius. Scripture says that he was too upset to eat, to have female company, or to sleep. At the first break of day, Darius cried out in an anguished voice "Daniel … has your God … been able to rescue you?" (v. 19). This pagan king had an inner longing to believe that Daniel's God might possibly be more powerful than a cave of starving lions. This says a lot about the witness of Daniel's life. He also had a strong "press."

# GAINING A FAITHFUL WILL

Our will, our feet, and our obedience must align with the heart and mind. No matter how much we love God with our hearts, or how much we believe Him with our minds, we must also *be willing to do the hard thing.* Daniel possessed the faithful will to do the hard thing. Being one with God was of more value to him than his physical life.

Dr. Joe Stowell, former president of Moody Bible Institute, was faced with this pressure to go undercover as a Christian. He was present at a prayer breakfast in Chicago where many faiths were represented, but no one—not even the Christians—mentioned the name of Jesus. He recalls that the message was very clear: All the "gods" were to be equal. The speaker said that they must give up the things "that divide us." This meant that the "Only-Way-Jesus" didn't fit in.

When the message was finished, everyone stood in boisterous applause. But Joe says, "I felt awkward. Awkward and alone. For the first time in my life, I was being asked to publically deny Jesus"—to go undercover, to conceal his beliefs and to keep Jesus to himself as a private matter. "At that breakfast I made a decision … to stick up for Jesus whenever and wherever." Thus he refused to stand.[4] When he turned his head, he saw that the entire Moody faculty present that morning had made the same choice to remain seated.

Isn't this also an awesome scene to imagine? I hope that each one of you knows someone right now who stands this boldly for God without compromise against a cultural horizon that tolerates every form of impurity imaginable. And I know that deep down you admire them greatly and wish you could be more like them. God is already using them in your life right now.

Your will is the part of you that makes the choice to actually obey God and live out, for all to see, that your identity is in Christ. In our country, the greatest price you may have to pay is losing a friend or receiving ridicule from those who don't understand. It's a sad thing to fear the loss of social approval more than the loss of God's approval. People have died for us to have the legacy of faith we have today. They did not fear them; the possibility of death was not nearly as disturbing as the possibility of a compromised life.

While the threat of death was not enough to stop Daniel's prayers, for most of us busyness alone is enough to stop ours. Absorption with our own agendas becomes a ruling habit, a way of life. However, the actual issue is not my busyness. It is whether or not my daily life, heart, mind and will belong to Jesus Christ. Anytime I fail to put God in His rightful place, the rat race will always overtake me.

The pressures in your lives will never be less than they are right now. Today is the time to make the hard decisions about your priorities. Prayer, worship, and study of His Word will show you how to know God in a personal, intimate way. You can pour out your hearts before Him, learn to be still and listen for His voice, His viewpoint. Knowing Jesus personally will transform you from within.

## BREAKING THE PRESS

Suddenly, breaking forth into the still gray dawn came the voice of Daniel rising to proclaim, "My God sent his angel, and he shut the mouths of the lions. They have not hurt me" (v. 22).

King Darius was beside himself with joy. Immediately he ordered Daniel to be lifted from the den to discover that "no wound was found on him, because he had trusted in his God" (v. 23).

Subsequently, all those who had sought to destroy Daniel were brought to the den, thrown in, "and before they reached the floor of the den, the lions overpowered them and crushed all their bones" (v. 24). This is to let us know there was nothing wrong with the lions! They were not tame, toothless, or well-fed.

The final word on this story is that "Daniel prospered" (v. 28).

Just one man, now old and stooped with age, outlasted the entire Babylonian empire and won over the Persian King Darius who said, "I issue a decree that in every part of my kingdom people must fear and reverence the God of Daniel" (Daniel 6:26). He exalted and honored his Lord despite the intense pressures to cave. Because inside himself he possessed the personal confidence that God was in control and takes care of His own.

## WHAT IS GOD CALLING YOU TO DO?

The vast majority of people do not believe these stories are true, or if they are, things like this only occurred in biblical times. They would

consider any other viewpoint to be uneducated. In reality, it is they who
are spiritually illiterate and blind

In 1955 a young woman, Neng Yee, lived in Shanghai, China. She
was brought before communist interrogators pulsing with hate. They
screamed and slapped her around. "Now you will answer 'yes' or 'no':
Are you a Christian?" Her response was, "Yes! Oh, yes!" I cried out joy-
fully, enthusiastically. Yes, I am a Christian!" At that reply, the soldiers
were instructed, "Take her out and shoot her!"

In the courtyard she saw a wall pockmarked with bullet holes. There,
she was given a second chance to deny her God but refused even though
she was pregnant.

"'Fire!' Guns exploded; bullets cracked; chips of bricks stung my arms
and back. I collapsed to the ground. Was this all there was to dying?"

Later, the soldiers said they had been blinded by a bright light and
were unable to see their target. Neng Yee was released and eventually
spent the rest of her life as an evangelist in China and the United States,
leading thousands to know Jesus Christ.[5]

We are called to uphold the standard of God in a corrupt world, to
stand for truth despite the consequences. Like Darius, people without
faith long to believe that God is real, that He takes care of His children,
and that He will be faithful to His promises. The repeated questions I
hear from Christians are, "Can God really be trusted? Does He really
have power to help me? Does He really care?" Daniel's life dispels these
doubts.

## WANTED:

Christians who will say to frightened people today: "You do not have
to crumple under the pressures of life around you! The same power that
was available for those four young Hebrew men is still available for you
today because 'Jesus Christ is the same yesterday and today and forever'"
(Hebrews 13:8).

Here is the clear commitment of the great Jonathan Edwards, an 18th
century American minister, theologian, and missionary:

Resolved: To follow God with all my heart.

Resolved also: Whether others do or not, I will.[6]

Daniel and his friends were able to successfully break the press. They prospered because their corresponding inner pressure was greater than the outward pressures that came at them. *"Greater is he who is in you, than he who is in the world"* (1 John 4:4 KJV).

And that's a fact.

[1] Jay Kesler with Tim Stafford, *I Never Promised You a Disneyland*, Word, 1976, 54.

[2] Kesler, 79.

[3] Elisabeth Elliot, "Gateway to Joy," radio broadcast.

[4] Joseph Stowell, *The Trouble with Jesus*, Moody Publishers, 2003, 14, 22–23.

[5] Nora Lam with Richard Schneider, *China Cry*, Thomas Nelson Publishers, 1991, 128, 130–131.

[6] Jerry White, *The Power of Commitment*, NavPress, 1985, 18.

# CHAPTER 12

# GAINING GROUND IN TOUGH TERRAIN
### *"The Heart that Hurts"*

*I have told you these things,*
*so that in me you may have peace.*
*In this world you will have trouble.*
*But take heart! I have overcome the world.*
**JOHN 16:33**

T he hills of East Tennessee provide a challenging terrain for cross-country runners. One school is known for its "killer hill" near the end. Many athletes who run well fall behind on this steep terrain.

While the accounts of Daniel's deliverance and that of his friends are amazing and inspiring, they do provoke some questions: "What if they hadn't been delivered?" Why do such bad things happen? Why do good people suffer? I'm afraid to trust God. Is it possible for a person to do exactly what God wants him to do and still have things go terribly wrong?"

No sooner do we plunge enthusiastically into faith than we come upon a killer hill and find ourselves panting out such questions. All who follow Jesus on the narrow road will sooner or later stub a toe on the harsh issues of suffering, pain, and evil.

## WHEN THINGS GO WRONG

In Alabama, during a Palm Sunday worship service, the minister looked down with pride at his young daughter, who was seated on the

front row waiting to sing a special song. Suddenly, to the horror of everyone, a tornado came ripping through the small sanctuary, killing 16 people.
That precious daughter was one of them.

A driving accident in South Carolina took the life of a high school
girl. The next evening as her classmates gathered at the funeral home,
another student was tragically hit and killed by a car as he was leaving.

A member of the high school football team in our community was
driving to school when he noticed a man with car trouble on the side
of the road. He stopped to help. While he bent over a tire, the driver of
a pickup had a seizure that caused his truck to smash into the student,
nearly severing his left leg. The football player did not lose his life, but did
lose his leg.

Did God turn to an angel and say, "Oh, no! Look what happened"?
Situations like this can lead us to despair if we conclude that a God who
would allow this to happen can't possibly be loving or fair. We can be
devastated by raging emotions.

I recently called a veterans hospital and the recording offered nine
options. Number two was the suicide hotline. This is tough terrain with
no quick fixes. When suffering occurs, the pain in our heart can suck the
life out of us.

## FACING THE HILLS

Our son's cross-country coach always required the team to run the
actual course before a meet. It could be blustery, cold, rainy, or far away
but she knew that to succeed they had to learn the terrain, especially the
tricky and difficult parts. Likewise, it is essential to learn the ways our
enemy might use to bring us down. Whether big or small, the most accurate definition of suffering I have heard is "either wanting something that
I don't have, or having something that I don't want."[1]

## IDENTIFYING THE LIES OF SATAN

**1. Satan's Lie:** "If you were a better Christian, and had more faith, this
wouldn't have happened."

Satan will taunt us with this lie. But what about the minister whose
daughter was killed in church? Did he lack faith? Or the high school boy

killed at the funeral home? Had he secretly done something bad that God decided to punish him for?

Satan always wants you to doubt our worthiness in Christ. "God must be punishing me. What did I do wrong? If I had more faith, I would have a success story like Daniel. I must not be doing His will."

## A SIMILAR STORY

The book of Acts records the story of a young man named Stephen. He had such tremendous faith that Scripture describes him as "brimming with God's grace and energy ... doing wonderful things among the people" (Acts 6:8 MSG). Filled with the Holy Spirit, Stephen was chosen to be a leader in the early church. A persuasive debater and leader, he possessed great wisdom and faith. He captured the attention of people, winning them to Jesus Christ. You couldn't find a more spiritual young man!

Yet he was not delivered from suffering. At the prime of his life, he was ruthlessly stoned to death.

> **Truth is...**
>
> Satan always wants you to doubt your worthiness in Christ.

"Now, was Stephen's faith not sufficient? ... Were the prayers of all the multitudes of believers inefficient for some reason? ... We know the stones hit Stephen ... he felt pain ... Stephen died. His body lay dead in the street, inert and bleeding. Was this a total victory for Satan, for the unbelieving enemies who had organized the attack? As Stephen called out for help, did God not answer him? What really happened?"[2]

**God's Truth:** God will not leave you in despair. His Word provides the strength needed to help you cope.

Jesus talked straight to His disciples: "In this world you will have trouble" (John 16:33). Peter tells us not to be surprised when we encounter trials and not to view them as strange or unusual (1 Peter 4:12). James says to be joyful when we encounter trials of any sort because they help us to grow in our faith (James 1:2–4).

Christians are not exempt. Stephen was in the *center* of God's will, doing exactly what he had been called to do, but this did not spare his suffering. In fact, it was his powerful zeal that got him in trouble with the rigid Jewish leaders. His fearless faith was causing the new church to grow and they wanted to get rid of all Christians.

When they tried to publicly discredit him, it only angered them more for "they could not stand up against his wisdom or the Spirit by whom he spoke" (Acts 6:10).

But God has promised that while we are going through a trial, He will keep us from the *evil* contained within the trial (Psalm 121). Since this cannot mean that we will never get sick, be injured or die, what does it mean? That "no injury, no illness, no accident, no distress will have evil power over us, that is, will be able to separate us from God's purposes in us."[3]

This same idea is expressed in Romans 8:38–39, where Paul lists all the things that cannot separate us from the love of God: death, life, angels, demons, any power, height, depth, or anything else in creation.

Is this really possible? Or is it just religious babble? We catch glimpses from biographies like *The Hiding Place* by Corrie ten Boom, a Christian sent to a concentration camp for smuggling Jews out of Holland during World War II.

Corrie's sister Betsie spoke these words in a frail voice as she was dying, "Must tell people what we have learned here. We must tell them that there is no pit so deep that He is not deeper still. They will listen to us, Corrie, because we have been here."[4] How astounding to read how they did not allow the evil around them to enter inside their hearts! Because they endured triumphantly, their story has brought immeasurable comfort to those who suffer, and untold numbers of people have come to Jesus Christ through Corrie's story.

While things may not always go the way we plan, nothing can prevent the triumph of God's purposes over evil in any given circumstance when we turn it over to Him.

When suffering is in our lives, the evil would be to let it cause you to doubt God, to turn away from Him and to stop trusting Him. The evil would be to grow bitter, to lose faith and hope, to become resentful, angry, filled with despair or revenge.

Jesus said, "Be of good cheer, [take courage; be confident, certain, undaunted]! For I have overcome the world. [I have deprived it of power to harm you and have conquered it for you]" (John 16:33 AMP).

What awesome news! Jesus alone can offer us a security that can never be shaken. He alone has the authority to deprive Satan of the power to harm or conquer us.

**2. Satan's Lie:** "If God really cared, He wouldn't let this happen."

Satan always wants us to doubt that God is good, loving or fair. "Why trust Him? He has let me down!" Satan wants to stir up resentment in us so we will complain against God. He whispers, "If God really cared about you, He wouldn't let this happen."

However, Scripture, history, and the daily news reveal that God clearly allows evil to triumph temporarily. Pharaoh brutalized the children of Israel as slaves and Pilate was allowed to put to death the Son of God who had lived a blameless life. He also allowed the holocaust of the Jewish people before and after World War II, which subjected them to unspeakable atrocities. God has allowed school shootings, bullying, terrorist attacks, brutal murders, devastating earthquakes, and continual wars.

Yet even as these terrible events occur, we have God's promise that He is fully in control. He is not caught off guard or surprised. He says that not one sparrow falls without His knowledge (Matthew 10:29).

A situation occurred in my life that enraged me beyond measure. I was so angry that I intentionally left my Bible at home over a vacation. But after five days, surrounded by the beauty of the ocean, I yearned to hear from Him and deeply regretted leaving His Word at home. At 2 a.m. I started looking for a Bible in our rental house. Slim pickings! All I could find was a paperback copy of *Good News for Modern Man*.

Since I didn't want to try to "figure out" what God might want me to learn, I asked for His help and proceeded with the "open and point" method. I don't usually recommend—or use—this method, but I was desperate. This is reserved only for emergencies, and the key to this working is that you must stay where you land.

My heart sank. There before me was a stick figure drawing of Jesus before Pilate. "Okay Lord. Only You can make any sense out of this!" I read the passage but remained clueless. Closing the book, I meditated on the bizarre spot where my finger had landed.

Suddenly, as quietly as the surf creeps over the sand, God said to me, "Danielle, Jesus was never in the hands of Pilate. Pilate was in the hands of the Father. And you are not in the hands of those who have mistreated you. They are in My hands." Is that a staggering truth or what!

When we feel trapped by a situation or helpless in the face of some person or circumstance, we can remember that we are not in the hands of the trial, but the trial is in the hands of our Father. We can ask Him, "What do you want me to learn from this? What are You trying to teach me?"

**God's Truth:** The key to coping is how we choose to respond. In the midst of trying circumstances, Satan wants us to turn *on* God instead of *to* God. While God's desire is that nothing would separate me from His love, Satan's desire is to use everything he can to separate you from the love of God (Romans 8:38–39).

He is in us, with us, and for us. In John 11, Jesus wept at the grave of His friend who had died. Do you know that He collects every tear you have shed in His bottle (Psalm 56:8 TLB)? Do you know that your name is written on the palm of His hand (Isaiah 49:16)?

Could there be a safer place to be?

**3. Satan's Lie:** "There's an easy way to get rid of your pain."

When we're in pain we want to fight it, resist it, and grab the closest remedy.

**God's Truth:** Stephen faced this temptation. The high priest gave him a chance to defend himself and save his life. Instead he seized the opportunity to give an electrifying speech that exposed the religious leaders as a disbelieving group of people who throughout history had refused to accept the leaders God sent to them. The final blow was dealt when Stephen called them traitors and murderers.

Was this smart? He knew this would provoke severe punishment. Why didn't he just say what they wanted to hear so he could continue his work for God? For the sake of just a little compromise, he could have gone home to supper that night.

Satan will tempt you to deal with pain and anxiety in ways that will compromise our identity in Christ. People turn to the advice of friends and the remedies of the world to dull the pain. When we see the things people turn to besides God, we understand that they can become further traps of Satan. Whether it is substance abuse, materialism, work, play, lawsuits out of anger and greed, we can still find ourselves depressed, hard-hearted, and bitter.

This happened to a lovely Christian young woman, who by her own admission has an A type personality—never without her day planner and always in control. Upon graduation from college, many of her friends got married so she concluded she also needed a guy to be complete. She wanted something she didn't have. So she returned to a former boyfriend, fell on her knees crying and promised she would do anything to have him back.

Following him to another state, she began her new life. Yet with each passing day, her unhappiness increased. Within in a year, she again fell to her knees in tears. But this time it was to say to the Lord, "I will do whatever You want me to do." She came to the place where the only thing that mattered was God's plan for her life.

We must take our fingers out of the pie. I relinquish the way I desperately want things to be. I relinquish what I "have to have," the way I believe it "has to be," and how it "has to work out." I fully let go to place it in God's hands. I remain settled in my mind that His ways are higher than my ways (Isaiah 55:8–9), that His are best.

Today this young woman is a radiant, trusting, and married woman who boldly shares her story to help others wait for God's best.

Stephen, because of the power of the Holy Spirit within him, didn't fall into Satan's trap. With no shred of timidity or fear, he stood upright in the midst of overwhelming hatred and danger, declaring that the religious leaders had hard hearts and blind eyes.

"When they heard this, they were furious and gnashed their teeth at him" (Acts 7:54). They "went wild, a rioting mob of catcalls and whistles and invective" (MSG). Stephen then declared that he not only saw God in His full glory, but he also saw Jesus standing at His side (vv. 55–56).

**4. Satan's Lie:** "God has forsaken and forgotten you."

What kind of God would allow such an awful deed to occur to such an important leader? Couldn't God use him more if he lived a long life?

Stephen could easily have been torn apart by such thoughts. But his fate was settled. God did not intervene. He did not rescue or spare Stephen as He did Daniel and his friends. Outside of the city, the leaders removed their coats to move their arms more freely. Taking Stephen to a high place, they threw him down into a pit and hurled great boulders upon him until he died.[5]

To feel abandoned by God is perhaps the most devastating pain of all. Satan will do his very best to convince us that we have lost the loving care of the Father who we believed would always be there for us.

**God's Truth:** "I will never leave you nor forsake you" (Hebrew 13:5 PHILLIPS) is easier to read than to believe.

In 1971, a seventeen-year-old boy in Vietnam named Hien Pham was recruited to serve as a summer interpreter for evangelist Ravi Zacharias. Every time Ravi preached a sermon, Hien's eyes filled with tears and he would say, "Forgive me, brother. Can you give me a minute to enjoy the truth I just heard?" When they addressed a group of pastors, he put his hand on Ravi's shoulder and said, "Can I talk for just a minute?" Ravi never got to finish his message.

Hien Pham began to beg and plead with the leaders of his country to turn to God. He and Ravi said good-bye at the end of that summer.

In 1974, Hien joined the army and Vietnam fell. He tried to escape the country but was caught and put behind bars. In three different prisons he was tormented in mind and body. They tortured him for being a Christian, a CIA spy. Then an intensive brainwashing process began. They forced him to read communist books in Vietnamese by Marx and Lenin that deplored capitalism.

The more he read, the more he began to think that maybe the communists were right. Had the American missionaries lied? On the verge of breaking, he was given one final book that pushed him over the edge. He cried out, "God, I don't believe you anymore." The day that he abandoned God, he was put in charge of latrine duty, cleaning the dirty toilets in the camp.

Amid the stench, a small can held pieces of paper that had been used as toilet paper. When he went to empty it, he thought he saw English writing. As he looked closer he saw "Romans" written on the top.

Picking it up, he washed off the human excrement, put it in his pocket and returned to his room. There, near midnight in his mosquito net, he pulled out a flashlight and began to read:

"If God be for us, who can be against us? ... Who shall separate us from the love of Christ? Shall tribulation, or distress, or persecution, or famine, or nakedness, or peril, or sword? ... Nay, in all these things we are more than conquerors through him that loved us. For I am persuaded that neither death, nor life, nor angels, nor principalities, nor powers, nor things present, nor things to come, nor height nor depth, nor any other creature, shall be able to separate us from the love of God, which is in Christ Jesus our Lord" (Romans 8:31–39 KJV).

Away with Lenin! Away with Marx! In the net he bent his knee and gave his life right back to God in full surrender. The guards were using the Word of God for toilet paper. The next day he went back to the commanding officer and asked for latrine duty every day. While working there, he collected the whole book of Romans!

Later he was called before the guards. He was commended for an outstanding spirit, was cleared of CIA charges and released. Through intricate circumstances he found a way to escape and provide help for 54 other people. Just before putting his boat into the river, he was again challenged by two officials who demanded to know if he was trying to leave. When he felt he could not lie, he therefore replied "yes." They immediately grabbed him and asked to go with him! He later said that at one point those two men actually saved his life when he became weak and nearly died. Hien, now named Fahman, became a U.S. citizen in 1989 and is a successful business man in Dallas, Texas.[6]

**5. Satan's Lie:** "Why me?" is by far the most common response to pain. Why did my flight get cancelled, my car break down, my parents get a divorce?

**God's Truth:** How remarkable that Stephen never said those words. This tells us that his spirit was not rebellious but submissive—submissive to the sovereignty of God.

I attended a conference led by Elisabeth Elliot and the last hour was for questions from the audience. With each card, she read the situation:

"My son is on drugs ... my husband is having an affair ... my sister is an alcoholic ... I lost my job ... I have no money." After reading each card, she quietly laid it down, looked at the audience and steadily stated, "Well, the first thing you must do is accept this" and then gave some extra words of counsel. *Thirty* times she calmly repeated, "First, you must accept this."

I was stunned. What did this mean? That's too simple. Don't we need lots of different approaches to such diverse personal problems?

Though it has taken me many years to really "get it," I now understand. Too often when suffering hits, we fight it with resentment, self-pity, anger, unforgiveness, guilt, blame, and shame. We may turn on ourselves or someone else. Thus all the emotional and spiritual energy that could be used toward overcoming and healing is instead consumed by our inner protest: "This is not going the way I wanted it to go. I don't want to accept this circumstance. I don't like it."

## Get Real:

**True acceptance means I ask God's help not to say, "Why me?" but to ask instead, "Why not me?"**

Our neighbor loved to play high school football, but one day he developed a staph infection. The medication required to treat it ulcerated his entire colorectal system. The necessary surgeries extended over eighteen months and resulted in a totally new, surgically created, digestive system. Morgan was angry and filled with months of asking, "Why?"

But because his life was found in the Lord, he gradually began to relinquish his pain to God and to trust Him completely. Now a senior in college, he is on call for the Cleveland Clinic to give encouragement by phone to others facing the same procedures. He is pursuing a medical career is one of the most positive people I know!

True acceptance is *not* mere resignation or tolerance. True acceptance means we understand that the world is not fair, but fallen. It means I ask God's help not to say, "Why me?" but to ask instead, "Why not me?" True acceptance says, "Lord, I hate this. With all my being I wish it was different. But I do believe You are in control and that You want only the best for me. So because I trust You, I *accept* this pain, this disappointment, this tragedy, this illness, this loss, knowing that You alone can heal the hurts and bring good out of this suffering."

**6. Satan's Lie:** "Suffering is a senseless waste."

**God's Truth:** The bold affirmation of the psalmist in 119:91 says of God: "All things serve you." This means that in God's economy *nothing* is ever wasted. It is human nature to question whether or not God has clear judgment. What a "waste" we think when a godly young person or leader dies! Our first thought is that they could have done so much more good with a longer life. It is a tough truth to grasp but it will free you from overwhelming distress to understand that all tragedies, all atrocities *will* one day serve Him—because He has placed everything under His feet (Ephesians 1:22).

I have a friend who grew up in rural China. When she was 19, an angry young man threw acid over her face and shoulders. Because she required extensive surgery and mental rehabilitation, she was sent to Shanghai where she lived for nearly two years. It was there in the hospital that nurses shared Jesus Christ with her, and she came to know Him as Lord. Her first priority became leading her sister and mother to know Jesus also. She learned to speak English and became a servant in the home of a Christian family from my hometown that was living in China. When the family moved back here, Xiou Ai kept in touch with them and eventually came over for a visit. The deepest desire of her heart was to get married.

Some of my friends and I explained that the plastic surgeons in the States could likely perform more skilled work on her face. But Xiou Ai said, "No. Now instead, I want to focus on inner beauty." Eventually she married a Christian man in our community.

Today she and her husband have a vibrant prayer ministry here, as well as in China, as she spends many hours a day on Skype counseling those in need. And her face is so radiant, her eyes so bright with the love of Jesus that her beauty is overwhelming! She is now a representative for a cosmetic line. Her business card reads: "Two things can make you more beautiful, Jesus Christ on the inside and Mary Kay on the outside."

Stephen's story presents an interesting commentary. When the religious leaders saw Stephen, he was unlike anyone they had ever seen before because "his face was like the face of an angel" (Acts 6:15) as he spoke to them before his death.

Who made this observation? It is customary to conclude that Luke, the writer of Acts, was not present at the stoning.[7] Those who sat on the council were out to get Stephen, not to admire him. Yet someone reported this as a fact. Obviously, *the way he died* startled even the cynics. Stephen not only had the light of life, he died radiating that light. His last words were, "Lord, do not hold this sin against them" (Acts 7:60)—words nearly identical to those Jesus prayed on the cross (Luke 23:34).

That prayer echoed off the rocks that lay beside his battered, lifeless body. It echoed off a pile of coats that the executioners had tossed at the feet of another young man (7:58), the one the Bible says was "giving approval to the death" (8:1). But most of all, the prayer echoed endlessly in the head of that young man named Saul. He could walk away from the coats, the body, the rocks, but he could not walk away from the relentless resounding of those words that he carried within him: "Lord, forgive them," nor the image of Stephen's face as radiant as an angel.

With all his might, he tried to get away from those words. He became the chief ringleader for launching a ruthless tirade on all Christians, to exterminate anyone who named the name of Jesus Christ. Surely, that would still the resounding echo in his head.

Be sure to catch his name: Saul. It was Saul who stood with the coats piled at his feet, giving approval to the murder of Stephen. "On that day a great persecution broke out against the church ... [and] Saul began to destroy the church. Going from house to house, he dragged off men and women and put them in prison" (Acts 8:1–3).

**7. Satan's Lie:** "I have won."

It appeared that Satan had won. In his plot to exterminate the Christian movement, Satan presumed he has scored a big one and made a strategic inroad!

**God's Truth:** However, the trip to Damascus with its mission of destruction (Acts 9:1), would have taken approximately six days. "During those days Saul swayed in a saddle under the intense heat of the sun. Back and forth ... those words kept echoing ... how could Stephen have prayed to forgive him? ... Back and forth ... back and forth ... that face had shone like the face of an angel ... back and forth ... who was this Jesus anyway, the Jesus who Stephen had died for? ... Back and forth"[8]

Suddenly, a blaze of light outshining the sun poured out of the sky on Saul and his companions. Saul fell to the ground (Acts 9:4). Then he heard a voice saying, "Saul, Saul, why are you out to get me?" (v. 4 MSG). Envision the panic as Saul asks, "Who are you, Master?" (v. 5 MSG). And picture further the terrifying reality as the answer came: "I am Jesus, the One you're hunting down" (v. 5 MSG).

God, who allowed Stephen to die smack-dab in the middle of His will, had just made a personal arrest of the executioner.

But it was an arrest of love. Because on that dusty road on a day that split time, instead of receiving judgment or punishment or retribution, Saul received a personal revelation of Jesus Himself—and he was never the same again.

Not even his name stayed the same. It was changed to Paul. He became the greatest convert, missionary, preacher, and writer the Christian world has ever known. The Christian movement, which Satan had sought to exterminate, had just inherited the greatest leader ever given, the greatest spread of growth thus far, and some of the most inspiring scripture to ever be written. Over half of our New Testament was written by Paul and still ministers to Christians today.

Perhaps no other human being has had a greater impact on the Christian faith. Except for maybe one: a young man named Stephen—a guy whose life, though battered, was a road sign that clearly pointed a lost man to a new road where he met for himself "the light of life."

A guy with a very short life. Was it a senseless waste? So much potential. Did God let him down? Forsake him?

Hardly. Because, though battered, Stephen was a road sign. And road signs don't exist for themselves. It doesn't matter if the road sign is a big, shiny green one on an interstate, or a small beat-up road sign on a dirt road, as long as it points people in the right direction, they have fulfilled their purpose.[9]

We are not here for ourselves. The chief aim of life is likeness to Jesus.

It was Stephen's life that impacted Paul. Nothing impacts another life as powerfully as when others observe that a person who still loves and trusts God even under pressure. People take note of the way we deal with insult and injury. "Stephen clearly loved and trusted God in the midst of terrible affliction … The work which Stephen did in his death had greater effect upon history than simply a longer life."[10] While we all desire a long life, it is not the ultimate goal of the believer.

St. Augustine, born in AD 354, wrote, "If Stephen had not spoken thus, if he had not prayed thus, the church would not have had Paul."[11] When Saul saw the way Stephen died, the impact on Paul was so profound that he became the greatest Christian missionary the world has ever known. Stephen followed the example of Jesus to the very end.

## SO WHO WON?

Though battered, Stephen's life serves as an arrow on a road sign to designate which lane to follow. Life is not senseless because God is in control, and in the end all things do serve His purposes—even evil.

Joseph was able to say to his brothers who had mistreated him decades earlier: "You intended to harm me, but God intended it for good to accomplish what is now being done, the saving of many lives" (Genesis 50:20).

A verse we can stake your lives on declares that "all things work together for good to them that love God" was written by Paul in Romans 8:28 (KJV). That doesn't mean some things, some times. It means all things, all the time.

To react, to respond to a crisis as Stephen did in a God-sized way, means that no pain is lost, futile, senseless, or defeating. In God's economy, suffering is never senseless or wasted![9]

This is far beyond what the world can ever provide. When we're rooted in this reality, we will discover peace—a rare commodity today—and the unshakable kingdom that Jesus wants to give us (Hebrews 12:28).

Did Satan win out? Not on your life. Daniel's faith delivered him *from* suffering, defeated Satan, and brought glory to God. Stephen's faith delivered him *through* suffering, defeated Satan, and brought glory to God. Which one was greater?

Ah, you see. That's why Satan lost—both times.

Being a Christian is never immunity from difficulties, but victory in difficulties. Stephen was never in the hands of the angry religious leaders, but was always (and only) in the hands of God.

## KNOWING WHERE TO GO

The precious truths written here are easier to read than to do. I have known forms of distress that reduced me to nothingness, where I couldn't focus on words to pray or Scripture to read. I was unable to engage my faith. When this occurs, it is essential to know where to go. We go to the one who says, "Fear not, for I am with you. Do not be dismayed. I am your God. I will strengthen you; I will uphold you with my victorious right hand" (Isaiah 41:10 TLB).

God is much more than the answers we seek from Him. When we have no answers, His presence is enough. When all we can do is crawl into His lap as a tired child, we will be secure in the cleft of His rock. There we can rest in complete trust that He is our precious and all-sufficient cover, shelter, and provider.

The psalmist said, "You are my hiding place; you will protect me from trouble" (Psalm 32:7). As the old hymn says: "Rock of Ages, cleft for me; let me hide myself in Thee." Learn to hide yourself in the cleft of His protecting Rock and let Him be your hiding place "when the great waters [of trial] overflow, they shall not reach [the spirit in] him" (Psalm 32:6 AMP).

This is where Corrie ten Boom found the title for her book. "For I too had a hiding place when things were bad. Jesus was this place, the Rock cleft for me."[12] Every day as she suffered she prayed, "Will you carry this too, Lord Jesus?"[13] Not only does He carry our suffering, but "He always carries the heaviest end Himself."[14]

If change can be brought, pray for the situation to change. With confidence, come boldly before the throne of God "that [you] may receive mercy and find grace to help [you] in [your] time of need" (Hebrews 4:16). However, do not come with a demanding spirit of lust to have it go a certain way, but bring a yielded spirit of humility, accepting whatever God allows.

Here is a prayer that reflects this kind of acceptance:

"Lord,
I am willing to receive what you send
I am willing to lack what you withhold
I am willing to relinquish what you take

I am willing to suffer what you allow
I am willing to do what you command
I am willing to be what you require."[15]

One Sunday in church our son, then seven, spent the entire sermon time drawing a picture of the empty tomb. It showed the rock rolled away and a cross with a cloth draped over it. Across the bottom he wrote in big, bold letters "He Has Won." I had no idea where he had heard or seen that phrase. Yet somehow, within his young spirit, he understood the bottom line: Our God has already won.

"For the mountains may depart and the hills disappear, but my kindness shall not leave you" (Isaiah 54:10 TLB). But God's truth stands firm like a great rock, and nothing can shake it" (2 Timothy 2:19 TLB).

---

[1] Elisabeth Elliot, *A Path Through Suffering*, Servant Publications, 1990, 56.

[2] Edith Schaeffer, *Affliction*, Fleming H. Revell, l973, 33.

[3] Eugene Peterson, *A Long Obedience in the Same Direction*, Inter-Varsity Press, l980, 38.

[4] Corrie ten Boom, *The Hiding Place*, The Christian Library, Barbour Publishing, 1971, 211.

[5] F.F. Bruce, *The International Bible Commentary on The New Testament, The Book of The Acts*,WM.B. Eerdmans Publishing Co, 1986, 170-171.

[6] Ravi Zacharias, "Power for Living" magazine, Vol. 54, #2 SP Publications Inc.

[7] Ibid, Bruce, 172

[8] Lloyd John Ogilvie, "The Way of Getting on God's Agenda," Session 5 tape from *Drumbeat of Love*, Word, Inc., 1976.

[9] John White, *The Fight*, InterVarsity Press, 1976, 61.

[10] Schaeffer, 36.

[11] Ogilvie, 96.

[12] ten Boom, 166.

[13] Ibid, 190.

[14] Elliot, *A Path Through Suffering*, 31.

[15] Valerie Elliot Shepherd, "Gateway to Joy," radio broadcast.

# CHAPTER 13

# GOD DOES SPEAK
### "The Heart that Hears"

*I will instruct you and teach you in the way you should go;*
*I will counsel you and watch over you.*
**PSALM 32:8**

A t the men's NCAA basketball championship game in1993, an outstanding forward called a time out in a critical situation and received a technical foul. With only a little more than a minute left to play, he didn't realize there were no time-outs left for his team. While it may not have made a difference in the outcome of the game, it was devastating to the team, the coach, and to the player to get their "signals crossed."

In sports it's imperative to get correct signals. In a football game, the quarterback understands the play his coach has called. In baseball the pitcher carefully reads the hand signals of the catcher. Clear instructions between the athletes and the coach are essential.

While human coaches are flawed and subject to error, our heavenly coach, God our Father, always makes the right call and knows the signals we need. Since we will always be in need of God's guidance, the crucial question is: "Is it really possible for me to know God's will? How am I going to know? What are the signals? What if I get the signals crossed?" The good news is that we don't have to flounder in frustration or wander aimlessly when it comes to this question.

Since we know that God eagerly yearns to be in a relationship with us, we don't have to worry about whether or not He will guide and speak to us. He is not playing hide-and-seek, leaning over the windowsill of heaven, saying, "Betcha you can't find Me!"

We need to settle in our minds how eager God is to reveal His will to us. We don't have to twist His arm or plead with Him. It is the greatest desire of His heart to grant us His wisdom and to help us make decisions. Nothing is closer to His heart!

When the Hebrews traveled in the wilderness, God provided a pillar of cloud to guide them every day and a pillar of fire every night. When the pillars moved, they were to move; when the pillars rested, they were to stop.

God *never* left them guessing.

While these physical symbols will not likely show up in your front yard (although they could), today God primarily relies on His written Word (which they did not have then) and on His Holy Spirit (which had not been given yet). So if you feel like you are not receiving signals, it won't be because of God. He is always speaking to us! (Hebrews 1:1–2).

> **Truth is...**
>
> He is not playing hide-and-seek, leaning over the windowsill of heaven, saying, "Betcha you can't find Me!"

There is another essential requirement for hearing His signals: You must belong to Him. You must be His child, in His family, and "in His wallet" to get the signals straight. "He who belongs to God hears what God says. The reason you do not hear is because you do not belong to God" (John 8:47). The coach doesn't give his instructions to the people in the bleachers or on the other team. He only gives instruction to those on his team because they are his players—"because I will only reveal myself to those who love me and obey me" (John 14:23 TLB).

Next you must be willing to obey the guidance He provides. A coach can't work with the person who challenges his calls or walks off the court. We must be willing to submit to His ways. The signals are not nearly as hard to hear as they are to heed.

In order to be led, we must place ourselves in a teachable, submissive position. This is where we can get into trouble. It's hard to receive true

double-edged sword, it penetrates even to dividing soul and spirit, joints and marrow" (Hebrews 4:12).

He alone knew then that He had created me to be a Mary, just as He creates others to be "Marthas," and it is certain that this book would never have been written had I made a different choice. Others would be led differently since they have the gifts of service that Martha did.

**Mark:** He decided early on that he was looking for a girl who loved God with her whole heart. So he put himself in the places where he could meet that kind of person.

## SIGNAL # 3: Learn to Observe the Circumstances around You

Are they lining up in a specific direction? What doors are opening? What doors are closing? Could this be God speaking to you?

**Mark:** Around his junior year in college, he found himself attracted to a Christian girl at the same church he attended. As they became good friends, he knew he was very interested in her. However, there was one slight issue. Though Ann had been born and raised in the United States, she was of Indian descent.

Because of this, Mark decided to keep his silence and just observe her lifestyle for a time. If he saw that she placed her first identity with the Indian culture, then he felt it would not be wise to pursue her. Over time he was happy to observe that her interests were highly diverse. Her first identity was in Christ. So he made his move.

## SIGNAL # 4: Discern Who to Listen to. This Is Crucial!

As we mature, we need to become wise about whose advice we heed. Some people are only capable of giving the best of their human wisdom, which may or may not be in line with God's will for us.

In the same way that the Holy Spirit can highlight a Scripture, He can highlight the words of a person. Know which Christian friends and advisors God might use to help to you. We can recognize when God is using them to speak to us because we know the Holy Spirit lives within them.

For you, the best source of wisdom may be your parents. If they have genuine doubt about some of the choices you are making, it's wise to give due weight to their opinion. God may still lead you in a different direction, but parents are to be honored and respected.

Likewise, if a Christian whose life we respect raises questions about a direction we are taking, we need to listen carefully. Never base a final decision solely on human advice. But if God is truly guiding you, their words will line up with all the other signals. I know far too many people who ignored the counsel of those around them and as a result they reaped painful consequences.

**Mark:** One day, "out of the clear blue," a mentor called to talk. During the conversation he said he thought Ann might be a great girl for him to pursue. In fact, everyone they knew wholeheartedly supported their new relationship.

### SIGNAL # 5: The Inner Voice of the Shepherd

I know what you are thinking. "Okay, now she's really gone off into territory I don't understand. A shepherd? That term has no relevance to our culture!"

True, none of us likely have shepherds in our neighborhoods. But think of it this way: Have you had a favorite pet?

When we had cats, I concluded that a certain way of calling a cat (what we referred to as a "cat call") had a genetic component in our family. My husband and son had that "gene," but I didn't. The cat never came for me. One time "Dan the Man"—the cat—accidently, (of course), got caught in the fan belt of the car and, because he was hurt, he ran off to hide. It was only the call of our son that finally brought him home.

Jesus declared that when we belong to Him, we will learn to recognize His voice in the same way that our cat responded to my son's voice. Jesus described the relationship of the sheep to the shepherd this way: "The sheep listen to his voice. He calls his own sheep by name and leads them out. When he has brought out all his own, he goes on ahead of them, and his sheep follow him because they know his voice. But they will never follow a stranger; in fact, they will run away from him because they do not recognize a stranger's voice" (John 10:3–5).

This principle is illustrated beautifully in a story told by Lloyd Ogilvie. While visiting the Holy Land, in the evenings, he would take long walks along the hillsides, stopping to watch large flocks of sheep in the valley below. "As the sun began to set, I watched a remarkable thing take place. Suddenly, as if by some prearranged signal, the shepherds began to call out to the sheep. Each walked in a different direction. To my utter amazement, the sheep, after some milling around, divided, and a separate groups followed each shepherd … They knew their shepherd and he knew his sheep."[1]

Belonging to Jesus means that day by day you can acquire the ability to hear His voice more clearly. Amid the clamor of all the other voices vying for your attention, learn to turn your head to His voice. Then follow because "As for God, his way is perfect … [he] broaden[s] the path beneath me, so that my ankles do not turn" (Psalm 18:30, 36).

You may still be very confused, wondering if this means that Jesus will speak to us in an audible voice. While He could, He most frequently speaks as an inner conviction in our mind or heart that leaves a strong impression. Always wait for the "voice of the Shepherd" before making personal decisions.

There was a time in the past when situations at our church became quite stormy. The decision about whether our family should leave or stay consumed much thought and prayer. The facts regarding the circumstances would clearly have led us to leave. Family and friends said it was the only sensible thing to do. Several of our close friends did leave.

But the voice of the Shepherd told us to stay.

Now we know that had we left, we would have missed some of the most phenomenal blessings of our entire life as a family, especially our sons. There is no easy or fast formula for hearing the voice of the Shepherd because it only comes through a personal relationship with Him. But the inner voice is a highly significant signal. Don't pass "Go" without it.

As Paul, and many saints who have gone before us, have said: "Mind the checks." If there is a check in our spirit, God may be saying to wait or to stop. After all, only He knows the future and He "will perfect that which concerns me" (Psalm 138:8 NKJV).

**Mark and Ann:** Before long, they knew they wanted to be married. Neither one of them ever had any hesitancy. However, there was one final hurdle to overcome.

### SIGNAL # 6: The Safety Net

This last signal is the safety net for those still unsure about whether they're getting the signals straight.

To the best of your ability, following the principles listed above, you can make your decision, praying that if it is not the wisest path, God would close the door. Isaiah 30:21 says, "If you leave God's paths and go astray, you will hear a Voice behind you say, 'No, this is the way; walk here.'" That's a check.

One time I truly believed that all the signs had lined up to lead me in a certain direction. So I acted accordingly and began to live out the decision I had made. All of a sudden, with no warning, the door slammed in my face. Even though I was stunned and confused, I knew that it was God who had closed the door. He made His signal very clear.

Don't worry about the mess-ups! We all make them, but when we belong to Him, He whispers, "Gotcha covered!" With every decision, leave the provision that if it not be God's will that He will redirect your steps. He will not fail you!

**Mark and Ann:** What was the one hurdle? Since the Scripture does not give specific guidance about interracial marriage, they turned to the principle of honoring their parents. From her tradition, marriages are often arranged. Her parents had an arranged marriage. From our perspective, we did not know her at all.

Thus they both agreed that if even one of the four parents did not approve then they would not pursue marriage. That was quite a sacrifice on their part. But the full blessing of all four parents would be their final confirmation of guidance.

Before he could officially date her, he had to meet with her parents at their request for about two hours. They wanted to get to know him. One of their main concerns was the divorce rate in our western culture.

Again, happily, it didn't take long for all four parents to give full consent to their pursuit of marriage. As I write this, their second child has just arrived.

## BELONGING TO HIM

Think again about a favorite pet. To them your presence represents food, warmth, protection, comfort, and love. Likewise we can come to associate the Shepherd's presence in our lives with peace, joy, and provision. That's what relationship is all about. That's why the psalmist could proclaim that when we belong to Him, "I shall not want" (23:1 KJV). Why would anyone not choose to follow?

Phillip Keller, a Christian writer who spent many years as a shepherd in his homeland of East Africa, relates this powerful story:

When Keller was a young man he sought to begin his own sheep ranch with the purchase of a fine ram for sire. He was determined to keep only the finest stock and breed only the best sheep. He went to visit an elderly, white-haired breeder who was highly regarded for his top-notch animals. The old man told Keller to take his pick of the flock, but with great wisdom Keller recognized that only the owner would truly know which sheep was the finest. With this request, the old man swung open the gate and "quickly he caught hold of a fine, handsome ram with a bold, magnificent head and strong conformation.

"'This is Arrowsmith II,' he said … He has won all the top awards across this country! … He's my top prize ram … tremendously valuable … more than that … very precious to me in a very personal way!'"

Keller then shares this reflection: "I could understand exactly what he meant. I was not surprised to see a misty look steal across his eyes … That day it came home to me with great clarity that what made the difference between one sheep and another was the owner. In whose hand had they been? Who was responsible for breeding, raising, and shepherding them? Was it a grand flockmaster? Was it a superb sheepman?

"And so it is with us. Are we in God's hands? Who is handling us, shaping us? Whose are we? Whose life is molding mine?"[2]

John Wesley said it this way in a prayer: "O Lord, I am no longer my own but yours. Put me to what you will, rank me with whom you will; put me to doing, put me to suffering; let me be employed for you or laid aside for you, exalted for you or brought low for you; let me be full, let me be empty; let me have all things, let me have nothing; I freely and wholeheartedly yield all things to your pleasure and disposal. And now, glorious and Blessed God, Father, Son, and Holy Spirit, you are mine and I am yours. So be it. And the covenant now made on earth, let it be ratified in heaven. Amen."[3]

[1] Lloyd John Ogilvie, *The Bush Is Still Burning,* Word Books, 1980, 124.

[2] Phillip Keller, *A Shepherd Looks at The Good Shepherd and His Sheep,* Zondervan Publishing House, 1978, 185, 18.

[3] The Methodist Service Book of the Methodist Church of England.

# CHAPTER 14

# A CHANCE TO DIE
## *"The Sacrificial Heart"*

*So I will very gladly spend for you
everything I have and expend myself as well.*
2 CORINTHIANS 12:15

In baseball, there is a play called the sacrifice bunt or fly. The batter deliberately intends to be called out at first base. The purpose of this play is to advance the runner on second base. While the batter is personally called "out," he is actually advancing the team.

The title of this chapter is taken from a biography of Amy Carmichael, a young Irish girl who accepted God's call to become a missionary at age eight.[1] Her love for Jesus compelled her to go to South India in 1895 at the age of 28. An older missionary spoke some words to her that stayed with her for life. When she remarked about something that was not to her liking, he replied, "See in it a chance to die."[2] She devoted the rest of her life to establishing a refuge for children who were being sacrificed as prostitutes to pagan gods. Her profound writings lift us to a level we rarely hear about today.

God also began speaking to me at age eight, but it was not to go to a foreign country or to be a missionary. I simply became aware of His presence and knew He was real in a personal way. I share this because many of you may be thinking that Amy was unusual. In reality she was an ordinary person like you or me. But her understanding that every day we have a chance to die has been a great challenge to me since the moment I heard it.

It is a challenge I frequently fail. Dying to anything in me that does not represent the character of Jesus is hard. But I have reached the place where I would rather fail at trying to do God's thing than to succeed at doing my own. Paul said of himself, "I have been crucified with Christ". (Galatians 2:20). Our identification with Jesus also calls us to identify with His death. To be identified with Jesus is to accept His mission. We are here to advance His kingdom not our own.

Jesus told the story of a man journeying from Jerusalem to Jericho. Along the way he was attacked, robbed, and left half dead on the side of the road. (See Luke 10:30–37.) These robbers illustrate one way we can live:

**The Takers:** "What's yours is mine, and I'm going to take it."

This group takes what they want for themselves without any regard for others. If you, or someone you're with, pressures another person for sexual intimacy, takes advantage of another's feelings and reputation, or tarnishes the good name of someone else to get themselves off the hook, this would make you a taker. The takers will lie to their family and friends, shoplift from a workplace or store, copy someone else's work or plagiarize material from the internet.

Takers grab the biggest and the best, will use handicap parking spaces, violate speed limits, break into a line without waiting, take money from a parent or sibling without asking, borrow clothes without permission, waste another's time by being late, and litter the highways. They will vandalize the property of others, and by reckless or drunk driving perhaps harm another human being. On a larger scale takers will seek excessive lawsuits motivated more by greed than need.

You may be thinking, "Give me a break! Everybody does those things!" Yes, but that is exactly the point. Jesus said that many choose the broad road that leads to destruction. In contrast, each one of these situations can provide us with an opportunity to take the way of Jesus and choose to die to self.

In Jesus' story, eventually a priest came traveling down the same road. But choosing to ignore the wounded man, he passed by on the other side. Later a Levite traveled the same route. Levites were men of status and respected for their knowledge of God. He also passed on the opposite side.

The priest and the Levite illustrate another way we can live:

**The Keepers:** "What's mine is mine and you can't have it."

Because I have personally seen this road to Jericho, believe me, those guys had to hug a mountain to walk on the other side! These men reveal the second way we can live: They don't actually *take* what belongs to someone else, but they are very careful to *keep* what is theirs to themselves. This mind-set is a sly snare for Christians today. The most destructive danger from past history is indulgence in personal peace and prosperity. In his book *America and Americans* John Steinbeck gave this warning in 1966:

"Now we face the danger which in the past has been the most destructive to the human: success, plenty, comfort, and ever-increasing leisure. No dynamic people have ever survived these dangers."[3]

If you're a keeper, you likely enjoy your comfort, convenience, and pleasure and do not like for your personal agenda to be interrupted. You're especially possessive of keeping your time to yourself. Whether the vantage point is the computer screen, the iPhone, iPad, the couch, or the car, it's easy for us to go for weeks without ever encountering a suitemate, a neighbor, or any of God's children truly in need. What might it mean for us to die to some of our indulgences?

Some of us are also known for keeping track of the wrongs of others. If you tend to be a perfectionist, be aware that it can result in expecting those around you to be perfect. For you who are perfectionists, it will come very naturally to you to find fault in others. Please consider yourself duly notified: This is a toxic disease. Receive the opportunity to die to this as soon as possible.

The first two men who passed by were keepers. They had a knowledge of God that did not translate into a greater capacity for love and compassion.

"It is a tragic error to believe that one can be a Christian without being a follower of the Lord Jesus Christ ... Many erroneously believe they can come to Christ ... then walk away to continue living life as they please."[4]

**The Givers:** "What's mine is yours, and you can have it."

Finally, a man came along who was a Samaritan. He would have been despised because Samaritans were considered to be a mixed race of half-breeds. Yet, when he saw the beaten man, "he felt deep pity" (Luke 10:33 TLB). Kneeling down, the Samaritan bandaged his wounds by pouring on oil and wine, and he put the man on his donkey. He "walked along beside him till they came to an inn, where he nursed him through the night. The next day he handed the innkeeper [what is comparable to] two twenty-dollar bills … to take care of the man. 'If his bill runs higher than that,' he said, 'I'll pay the difference the next time I am here'" (Luke 10:33–35 TLB).

Jesus then said to His listeners, "Now go and do the same" (v. 37).

The Samaritan represents all those who are known as "the givers." You already know who they are, don't you?

## YOUR CHANCE TO DIE

I have a friend who stopped to help a family once on the side of the road, and that could well happen to you. However, what we see here is a new way of thinking. It means that each day will present us with the opportunity to depart from self through little "deaths."

It might mean yielding cheerfully to the wishes of someone else, doing a job without complaining, running an errand for someone, helping a sibling with homework, closing a door quietly instead of slamming it, being willing to turn down the volume on your music. It might be the willingness to keep quiet instead of sharing gossip or overlooking a slight from a friend instead of harboring a grudge. It could be as simple as releasing your viewpoint of things.

### Get Real:

Jesus instructs us to go and do the same as the Samaritan. Stop, bend down, serve, and expend yourself for the sake of others.

These are some of the subtle ways we can cling to self. But the exciting thing is that *every* time we submit our self-will on God's behalf, He *sees* the sacrifice and rejoices in our obedience to Him! It honors Him every time we willingly, not grudgingly, hold our tongue or go the second mile even when it's inconvenient. "A man's wisdom gives him patience; it is to his glory to overlook an offense" (Proverbs 19:11). Wow! Our choices will bless others and bring glory to Him.

The Samaritan died to his own agenda, his convenience, time, and money. Jesus instructs us to go and do the same. Stop, bend down, serve, and expend yourself for the sake of others.

## BECOMING HIS SERVANT

Jesus calls us to sacrifice without analyzing the cost to self, to become a "what's mine is yours" kind of person. He explained His own life by saying, "The Son of Man did not come to be served, but to serve" (Mark 10:45).

The sacrificial heart says, "You can have my time, my money, my pleasures, my comforts, and my conveniences. I freely give my energy, my talents, my intellect, my personality to God to be used by God for His purposes. I yield my 'rights'—my right to do things my own way, my right to pursue benefits only for personal gain, and my "right to be right."

As a career journalist, Philip Yancey, shares about his opportunities to interview great stars, athletes, musicians, and TV personalities who dominate the media:

"We fawn over them, poring over the minutiae of their lives; the clothes they wear, the food they eat, the aerobic routines they follow, the people they love, the toothpaste they use. Yet I must tell you that, in my limited experience, I have found ... our 'idols' are as miserable a group of people as I have ever met ...

"I have also spent time with people I call 'servants.' Doctors and nurses who work among the outcasts, the leprosy patients in rural India. A Princeton graduate who runs a hotel for the homeless in Chicago. Health workers who have left high-paying jobs to serve in a backwater town of Mississippi. Relief workers in Somalia, Sudan, Ethiopia, Bangladesh, and other repositories of human suffering. The PhDs I met in Arizona, who are now scattered throughout jungles of South America translating the Bible into obscure languages.

"I was prepared to honor and admire these servants, to hold them up as inspiring examples. I was not prepared to envy them ... the servants clearly emerge as the favored ones, the graced ones. Without question, I would rather spend time among the servants than among the stars: they possess qualities of depth and richness and even joy that I have not found elsewhere."[5]

## WHAT IF I GET RIPPED OFF?

The short answer is: You will! People will take your money, your time, your kindness. But that is between them and God. Between you and God is your obedience. Certainly we are to use reason and judgment, but we are not called to calculate. We are to pour ourselves out on behalf of others. No one was ever ripped off more than the Lord Jesus who, while perfect, died on a cross like a criminal.

A good friend of mine came to church one morning and said, "I want you to know why I wasn't here last week." She had instead been visiting her daughter's boyfriend at the county jail. This was not easy and did not come naturally, but when her prodigal daughter asked if she would visit him, she knew that God wanted her to go. This is what it means to be identified with Him. Our human nature will recoil every time and will rationalize by saying, "This doesn't apply to me." Becoming a giver does not come easily to our fallen humanity. We are not alone as is shown in this prayer by a devout Catholic priest:

"Lord, why did you tell me to love all men, my brothers?

I was so peaceful at home, I was so comfortably settled.

It is well-furnished, and I felt cozy ... clean ... my ivory tower.

I did not know they were so near ... my neighbor, my colleague, my friend. As soon as I started to open the door, I saw them, with out-stretched hands, anxious eyes, longing hearts, like beggars on church steps ...

You would have been pleased, Lord: I would have served and hon-ored you in a proper respectable way ...

But the next ones, Lord ... I had not seen them ... they overpowered me without warning.

They are in the way, they are all over ... I can't stand it anymore! It's too much! It's no life!

What about my job? My family? My peace? My liberty? And me? Ah, Lord! I have lost everything; I don't belong to myself any longer; there is no more room for me at home."

At the end of the prayer the priest pens a reply from God:

"Don't worry, God says, you have gained all,

While men came in to you,

I, your Father

I, your God,

Slipped in among them."[6]

## THE EXCITING NEWS

Nothing given for Him will *ever* be wasted. While Jesus and His disciples were at a dinner party, "a woman [identified in John's account as Mary, Lazarus' sister] came to him with an alabaster jar of very expensive perfume, which she poured on his head as he was reclining at the table" (Matthew 26:6–7). The disciples scolded her for wasting her precious perfume to anoint Jesus (vv. 8–9) They "calculated" commercially that it would have been more profitable to sell the ointment and use the money for the poor. But Jesus said, "I assure you that wherever the Gospel is preached throughout the whole world, this deed of hers will also be recounted, as her memorial to me" (Matthew 26:13 PHILLIPS). Why did the Lord say this?

"Because the Gospel is meant to produce ... our 'wasting ourselves' upon him. Have you ever given too much to the Lord? May I tell you something? ... In divine service the principle of waste is the principle of power. The principle which determines usefulness is the principle of scattering."[7]

Within the next couple of days, Jesus was crucified. Strict Jewish rule required a dead body to be anointed, but this could not be done for Jesus because the Sabbath began at sunset.

**Truth is...**

**Nothing given for Him will *ever* be wasted.**

That's why early in the morning of the third day, women went to the tomb to perform the ceremonial rite. But they could not because Jesus was not there. He had risen ... as He said!

The only person who succeeded in anointing the Lord was Mary. And she did it *before* the crucifixion because God told her to..

## LAVISH PEOPLE

"Have we come to see that nothing less than the dearest, the costliest, the most precious, is fit for him."[8] We are to be lavish in our love for God!

Some friends of ours loaned their minivan to another adult to drive some kids to camp. While there, local vandals broke into the camp and then began to throw bricks through the windshield of the minivan.

Although this was not a pleasant experience, the camp insurance covered all expenses to repair the van. So what were they really out? A couple of days and a little inconvenience?

But a teen was saved—ushered into eternal life!

Every time I pass that van on the road I think, "There's that blessed van, just as vital as the donkey Jesus had need of!" Because that hunk of metal advanced Jesus and His kingdom "further down the road."[9] My friends are sacrificial givers who lost nothing.

What do you have that He could use? He can take hold of whatever you can do and says, "Do it for Me." Our God is extravagant. And we are to be just like Him.

## THE LAST SHALL BE FIRST

A great story is told by Ed Beck, former basketball star and United Methodist minister.

Just prior to the summer Olympics in 1988, he visited the training center for the Olympic athletes in Colorado Springs where he lives. Thinking that he might find an illustration on the importance of community, he was disappointed. These marvelous athletes were simply too competitive.

Then the "Special Olympics" came to town. They were held at the Air Force Academy. Beck described the 100-yard dash.

"As the gun went off some of the runners were fairly fast and immediately left the rest behind. Others were moving little better than a walk. Suddenly, about 50 yards down the track, one of the runners in the main pack fell. Immediately, the entire race stopped. Even those who were close to the finish line returned to their fallen friend and gathered around shouting: 'Are you all right? Are you all right?' The one fallen responded: 'No! I'm not all right; I hurt!' At that point a beautiful thing happened.

"One of the runners knelt down, brushed off the scrape, kissed it and helped the injured runner to his feet. At that point they all held hands determined to restart the race from the middle of the track. As they looked back and forth at each other they all shouted: 'Are you ready? Are you ready?' at which point the gun went off again and they all started to run but they forgot to let go of the hands of the ones next to them so they all finished the race together ... they all finished last, and they all finished first because no one lost; and everyone won."[10]

Even though you may be one of those who can readily shine and quickly sprint ahead of all the others, would you stop, turn around, and help the ones behind you who aren't quite so quick, so cool, so adept? Is the purpose of life to be the first, the fastest, or to advance the kingdom of God? Jesus said "But many [who are now] first will be last [then], and many [who are now] last will be first [then]" (Mark 10:31AMP).

He calls us to find ourselves by losing ourselves. This isn't optional for the Christian; it is essential: "This is how we know what love is: Jesus Christ laid down his life for us. And we ought to lay down our lives for our brothers. If anyone has material possessions and sees his brother in need but has no pity on him, how can the love of God be in him? Dear children, let us not love with words or tongue but with actions and truth. This then is how we know that we belong to the truth" (1 John 3:16–19).

## A PIERCING STORY

Another glimpse from Corrie ten Boom:

"As the cold increased, so did the special temptation of concentration-camp life: the temptation to think only of one's self. It took a thousand cunning forms. I quickly discovered that when I maneuvered our way to the middle of the roll-call, we had a little protection from the wind. I knew this was self-centered: when I stood in the center someone else had to stand on the edge. How easy it was to give it other names!

"Selfishness had a life of its own. As I watched Mien's bag of yeast-compound disappear, I began taking it from beneath the straw only after lights-out, when others would not see and ask for some ... The cancer spread ... Was it coincidence that joy and power imperceptibly drained from my ministry? ... And there it was ... I could no longer separate ... the real sin ... I closed the Bible and to that group of women clustering close I told the truth about myself—my self-centeredness, my stinginess, my lack of love. That night real joy returned to my worship."[11]

Corrie didn't have to share this story about herself, did she? No one would ever have known this about her except the Lord ... But aren't we glad she did? Because each of you reading this is saying, "That's me," including myself. The exciting part is that every day, regardless of where we are or what we're doing, we can let ourselves decrease so He can increase (John 3:30).

German-born Dietrich Bonhoeffer was one of the most influential Christian theologians of the 1900s. While he could have taken refuge in the United States during World War II, he chose instead to remain in Germany to stand against Hitler.

The opening sentence of his great work, *The Cost of Discipleship*, attests to what is truly means to be a disciple: "When Christ calls a man, He bids him to come and die."[12]

The Nazis hanged him in 1945 at the age of thirty-nine. And yet he lives ... for more than seventy years, he continues to speak boldly and without apology to each new generation. He "wasted" his life for the Savior, and we are all better for it.

---

[1] Elisabeth Elliot, *A Chance to Die*, Fleming H. Revell Company, 1987, title page.

[2] Elisabeth Elliot, *A Lamp For My Feet*, Servant Publications, 1985, 29–30.

[3] John Steinbeck, *America and Americans* (1966) used in the "American Adventure Presentation," Epcot Center, Walt Disney World, Buena Vista, Florida, October 1987.

[4] John MacArthur, *The Gospel According to Jesus*, Zondervan, 1988. Foreword by James Montgomery Boice, xi .

[5] Philip Yancey, *The Jesus I Never Knew*, Zondervan, 1995, 117–118.

[6] Michel Quoist, *Prayers*, Sheed, Andrews, and McMeel, 1963, 117–119.

[7] Watchman Nee, *The Normal Christian Life*, Tyndale House, 1977, 275–276.

[8] Ibid, 279.

[9] Max Lucado, *And the Angels Were Silent*, Multnomah, 1992, 54.

[10] Robert G. Tuttle, *Sanctity Without Starch*, Bristol House Ltd., 1992, 157.

[11] Corrie ten Boom, *The Hiding Place*, The Christian Library, Barbour Publishing, 1971, 208–209.

[12] Dietrich Bonhoeffer, *The Cost of Discipleship*, A Touchstone Book published by Simon and Schuster, 1959, Foreword, 1.

# CHAPTER 15

# HERE AM I, LORD; SEND ME
## *"A Heart for the Lost"*

*He who has the Son has life; he who does not
have the Son does not have life.*
### 1 JOHN 5:12

I t's not enough to run the race. You must also pass the baton.[1] The relay runner has one purpose: a clean, firm handoff. He knows that the most critical part of the race is the transfer of the baton. It can slip, drop, or cause a runner to stumble.

We also have a clear purpose: a firm transfer of the Gospel. We must not be timid, slack, or lose our grip on truth. The heart of God is to reach the lost. "For God so loved the world that he gave his one and only son" (John 3:16). And why? Because "he who has the Son has life; he who does not have the Son of God does not have life" (1 John 5:12). Those we know who do not have the Son will have neither a spiritual life here nor an eternal life in heaven.

It was a bitter cold night in February as I sat among 3,000 people for Founder's Week at Moody Church in Chicago. That night they were honoring the alumni. I was astounded that so many in their 70s had come downtown on such a frigid night. One by one they stood to say the year they graduated and how long that they had been in ministry. There were missionaries who had served forty-five years, forty years, thirty-five years, and on and on. They continued down to the newest alum who had just served his first year.

There were also alumni who were not present because they were present with the Lord, even young ones who had sacrificed their lives to pass the baton. Here is the prayer that alumni Betty Scott Stamm wrote in 1925 at the age of nineteen:

"Lord, I give up my own purposes and plans, all my own desires and hopes and ambitions and accept Thy will for my life. I give myself, my life, my all utterly to Thee, to be Thine forever. I hand over to Thy keeping all of my friendships; all the people whom I love are to take second place in my heart. Fill me and seal me with Thy Holy Spirit. Work out Thy whole will in my life, at any cost, now and forever. To me to live is Christ. Amen"[2]

"At any cost" came to mean losing her life, as well as her husband's life, three years later in China. Miraculously, their three-month-old daughter was rescued by the underground church. The seeds of their sacrifice spread like wildfire in the United States, igniting hundreds of young people to respond by also saying, "Lord, send me."

## A LEGEND

There is a legend that when Jesus returned to heaven he bore the marks of abuse, anger, and scars from the crucifixion.

"The angel Gabriel stops Him saying, 'Master, you must have suffered a lot. It must have been horrible.

"The Savior looked deeply into the eyes of the angel and said, 'Yes I did and yes it was.'

"The angel continued, 'Do people now realize how much you love them, how forgiven they are, do they know what you did for them?

"Jesus said, 'Well, a handful know—a few—Peter, close followers like James and John and others. They know, they believe and now understand. Through them there will be others who believe and the message will continue on. I have left them with the great commission and they will carry it out.'

"But Gabriel was troubled. He continued, 'What if those who hear and believe don't tell what they've heard? What if they don't realize what a great commission it is? What if they, like in the 20th and 21st centuries, get involved in other pursuits and passions and go in the other direction and for some reason this great commission, well, you know, becomes the work of a few professionals? Do you have another plan?'

"Abruptly Jesus answered, 'There is no other plan. I have no other option but this one. I've provided them with the Holy Spirit, and eternal life through my blood, and have commissioned them to take the message to their world. That's the only way people will hear.'

"Do you remember the one who told you? A parent? A coach? A peer? What lengths did they go to for you? What lengths will you commit to the Lord? And now that you've heard, now that you understand, now that you know that this is what life is really all about, you are telling others, aren't you?"[3]

## THE GREAT COMMISSION

Jesus said to His disciples, "As the Father sent me, I now send you" (John 20:21 NCV).

*All* Christians are called to tell others about Jesus. That is the only way the lost can know how to enter the kingdom of God. I never say, "I just try to live my faith." First, because I am a very fallen, imperfect human being, which means I fail every day. Secondly, because Jesus is what people need, not me. It has been said, "If you meet me and turn away, you have lost nothing. If you meet Jesus and turn away, you have lost everything."

The person who reached me did not go into full-time ministry. She was a high school cheerleader with a red hoodie who stood up at a youth campfire to say she had met Jesus. Just think: God used a seventeen-year-old girl to hand me His baton!

I have a special friend who had a one-day, two-night honeymoon. On the second day of her life as a married woman, she was in a camper truck hauling a boat to Nicaragua where her husband was working through the University of Tennessee, School of Architecture. They were to live in Nicaragua for a year without electricity or running water. And there they fell in love with people who desperately needed Jesus—men who drank alcohol all day, women raising children with no diapers, clothes, or food, and children with no homes or school. As money allowed, they established a ministry and now live in the States only long enough to make more money for the ministry.

The theme verse for their ministry is, "Let them give glory to the Lord and declare *His praise* in the islands" (Isaiah 42:12 AMP). They do not do this in the name of humanity but in the name of Jesus. Their whole purpose is to introduce the island people to the Savior, not themselves.

God also used the ministry of Miss Mears, the lady with the funny hats, to call a young man named Jim Rayburn to leave his church job and take the Gospel straight to the high schools to reach teenagers. He was the founder of Young Life, a ministry that has also allowed countless kids to find life in Jesus Christ, now for more than seventy years.

What if Jim had waited for kids to come to him in Gainesville, Texas, instead of accepting God's leading to reach them on their own turf at school? From that one club in Texas in 1941, there are now clubs in *every corner* of the world. The baton is still being handed off one by one by one ... And if you count the people those people have impacted, you're looking at millions now found in Christ because of the obedience of one man.

Another young man reached through Miss Mears was a young guy named Bill Bright. What if, in 1958, he had ignored God's call to direct all his energies toward helping fulfill the Great Commission? Beginning with students at UCLA and in ministry for more than fifty years, Campus Crusade for Christ, now "Cru," is now in more than 190 countries with 250,000 trained workers seeking to reach the college population for Jesus Christ. One of our sons served in this ministry for more than six years.

When Mr. Bright died in 2003, his wife Vonette said, "If all Bill does is stand at the gate of heaven and welcome people who God saved through his ministry, that would keep him busy for a couple of centuries."[4]

Likely you have never heard of John Harper, who was born in 1872 and died in 1912. Sailing from London, he was on the Titanic the night of April 15th. When the crew realized the ship was sinking and there were not enough lifeboats, panic spread. The man responsible for the shortage crawled into a boat and left hundreds of women and children to drown.

But John Harper, a minister from Scotland, handed his only daughter over to her aunt and turned to the teeming masses behind him.

"Let the women, children, and the unsaved into the lifeboats!" he ordered. At 2:20 a.m., Harper and more than 1,500 others plunged into the icy waters as the ship broke in half.

As the lifeboats pulled away, "screams and cries for help began to fill the night air ... Concerned not for his life, but for the dying around him, Harper with his last breaths swam to the dying souls and cried out for them to be saved. 'Believe on the Lord Jesus Christ and thou shalt be saved!' As his strength began to ebb, Harper called out to a young man clinging to a piece of timber, 'Man, are you saved?' He replied 'I am not.'"

Harper gave the young man his life jacket saying, "Don't worry about me. I'm not going down. I'm going up ... Believe on the Lord Jesus Christ and thou shalt be saved!" Harper cried out one last time, and with that slipped beneath the waves for the last time.

Four years later, at a reunion of Titanic survivors, the young man, Aguilla Webb testified that he had been saved twice that night: once by the lifeboats, and the other by John Harper, saying, "I am John Harper's last convert."[5]

History documents that the lifeboats were only half full because those who were already safe would not return to those who were perishing. May this never be said of us! That we are "floating in our Jesus boats and they are only half filled! He expects you to turn around and go back to get someone else on board!"[6]

An old hymn says, "Rescue the perishing ..." If the life of Jesus in you is real, your heart will break for those who do not "have the Son." It will burn within you, and you will be compelled to go and tell of the life you now know firsthand. You will want to invest your life, your priorities, and your finances because nothing else will matter to you as much as telling others about Christ.

## Get Real:

> May it never be said that we are "floating in our Jesus boats and they are only half filled! He expects you to turn around and go back to get someone else on board!

Daily, our news is filled with people who have died tragically—children, young people, soldiers, and college students—and we as a country grieve deeply for them. I simply ask, "Do we grieve as deeply for those who are dying spiritually every day?" We take comfort in those in Christ who die because we know that they yet still live.

By contrast, we must grieve—as God does—over every lost person. Do you have this urgency? It is always urgent because one never knows how long a life will be, just like those people on the Titanic. I challenge each reader: Find your most effective way to reach the lost, to pass the baton. You can begin now to share the love of Jesus Christ through all your daily activities. You may be called to ministry or work for a mission outreach. Teach children, teach youth, and give money to those who are doing what Jesus would do!

David Livingstone was a Scottish explorer, who at the age of 28 was sent by the London Missionary Society to convert Africans to Christianity. He invested his entire life in ministry to the African people. Upon his death in 1873, there was a controversy regarding where he would be buried. The British wanted him buried in England since they were the ones who sent him to Africa. But Livingstone wanted his heart buried where he had invested his life.

The conflict was settled. His body was buried in Westminster Abbey, but, by his request, his heart was removed by his faithful servants in Africa and buried under a tree.[7]

Where would you want your heart to be "buried," invested? How awesome that our lives fully yielded and placed in God's hands will produce enormous harvests for His kingdom—forever. This means your life, yielded on behalf of others, will count for all eternity.

**Truth is...**

God's plan is for *your* life to impact eternity in a way that will be unique to you and for Him.

All of these people mentioned were just common, ordinary, everyday people like you and me. They are outstanding only because of how they allowed God to work *through* them. It's the same way with the people we've read about from in the Bible. People are given space in there only according to how they allowed God to advance His kingdom through them. That is why the rich young man is in five verses and Peter is in five books!

The best news of all is that anything God does through you will last forever. Is that awesome or what? Forever. After all, here we are now, still reading about these people, as well as the lives and writings of those who have gone long before us to obey Him. You see, God's plan is for *your* life to also impact eternity in a way that will be unique to you and for Him.

## WHAT YOU DON'T NEED

When I began my first job in the church, I knew nothing. I mean, really nothing, except that I loved God with all my heart and loved the kids in that church. That was all. And that was enough.

As I have shared, even with all my religious activities in high school, it took another young person to reach me. Right now you have a decisive door open before you to reach your peers before they begin a life without Jesus at the center. *No one can reach another young person like you can!* Shepherds don't produce sheep; sheep have sheep. It does not require great knowledge, training, eloquent speech, and certainly not a perfect life.

God gives you the priceless privilege of leading others to His light. It is astounding that from the beginning His plan has been to use normal, average or even less than average people to grow His kingdom! The priceless privilege of helping someone come to know Jesus and find life in Him is the greatest joy on earth. There is no deeper satisfaction than to be even a miniscule part of that plan.

The faces of the kids God has placed in my life scroll before me with love and joy. "Here am I Lord; send me" (Isaiah's response to God's call in Isaiah 6:8) is the way they live. Many of them have chosen to pursue full-time ministry, while others are taking their faith to secular jobs where they are surrounded by lost people. They are wonderful workers, husbands, wives, and parents. And they are teachers, counselors, and serving in the military. They are cosmeticians, entrepreneurs, culinary chefs, engineers, businessmen and women, doctors, and missionaries. Recently two "alumni" asked if they could pray with me about this book. And they are engineers. How cool is that?

There is much I do not know. But I do know that at age 18 God deposited a psalm song in my heart for the journey here and forever. "Better is one day in your courts than a thousand elsewhere" (Psalm 84:10). Do you understand and believe this? Of this I am absolutely certain: One day with Him *is* better than a thousand anywhere else. If I were playing football now, I would do a fist pump like the players do when they are ecstatic. Enthusiasm is contagious and there are multitudes around you in spiritual poverty.

I challenge you to live, not just marginally, but entirely for Him. Break from the pack! Get off the broad way of the herd and vehemently pursue the narrow road. Because life is not what it seems. What appears at first to be "broad" will getting narrower and more constricting, and what appears at first to be "narrow" will lead you to a life that is indescribable and immense, beyond all that you could ask or think.

Because this is where life is found.

... This is where you belong.

And here, you are not a tourist but a child at home.

One summer our family traveled through the mountains of West Virginia as we began a vacation. With pen and paper I was brainstorming with my "sports experts" to get ideas for this book. Since I had not discussed much about the content, our son John, who was ten at the time, asked, "What's the book about?"

"Well," I replied, "it's about what the goal of life really is."

Looking straight ahead, without even turning his gray-blue eyes, he very matter-of-factly said, "The goal is Jesus." That was one of those incredibly *better* days. Because our son had already received his hand-off. The baton was firmly secure in his hand. It doesn't get any better than that.

God commissions you to hand that baton of faith to those He has placed in your life, starting with your immediate family. Ask God to open your eyes to see those around you who are starving spiritually that they too can place their lives in His unshakeable kingdom.

Yes, John, the goal is Jesus.

---

[1] Kingdom Building Ministries Logo, Adrian Despres.

[2] Marvin Newell, *A Martyr's Grace*, Moody Publishers, 2006, 75.

[3] Chuck Swindoll, "A Legend," *Insight for Living*, radio broadcast.

[4] Vonette Bright with Lis Trouten, "God's Sustaining Presence," *Decision* Magazine, March 2009, Billy Graham Evangelistic Association, 17–18.

[5] Jim Ryun, *Heroes Among Us*, Destiny Image Publishers, 2002, 275–279.

[6] Dr. Tony Evans, Founders Week, Moody Bible Institute, February 4, 2005.

[7] http://en.wikipedia.org/wiki/David_Livingstone